THE HEALING HAND

5 discussions to have with the dying who are living

Sue Knight Deutsch

To Mimi and Jay,

Blessings to you!

Cantor Sue Knight Deutsch

i

Sue Knight Deutsch

Copyright © 2014 Sue Knight Deutsch

First printing, 2014
Printed in Korea

ISBN: 978-0-9908341-0-6

Library of Congress Control Number: 2014918202

Cover design: Charlotte Proud
Illustrations: Will Deutsch

Handutch Press
P.O. Box 3654
Mission Viejo, CA 92690

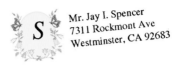

Mr. Jay I. Spencer
7311 Rockmont Ave
Westminster, CA 92683

In loving memory of my husband
Michael "Dutch" Deutsch
with whom I had these discussions
and who even in his death gave me a way
to move forward into life.

TABLE OF CONTENTS

THE HEALING HAND

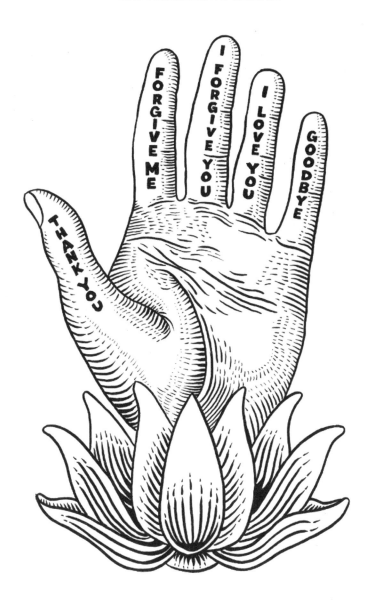

PREFACE: How to use this book

This is a book of questions that will engage you in conversation with yourself and others. It does not have all the answers. It is about what to ask so that you may find the answers that are uniquely yours. You already have the answers to these questions inside of you.

The picture on the previous page captures the essential information this book will provide you. After some initial discussion about the hand itself, the rest of the book is divided into five sections, each corresponding to one of the fingers on the hand, with a story, a question or a metaphor pertaining to that discussion. In addition, there are two appendices that follow, one pertaining to self-care, and one pertaining to the grieving process, which often begins long before the goodbye.

This book is intended to be by your side when I cannot be there with you. Though this book was originally intended to be used in the hospital room, my professional experience shows me that healing often takes place outside the hospital walls. Whether you are a professional or someone supporting a loved one who is ill, this book has something to teach as well as provide comfort and guidance. As such, it is not meant to be an academic tome—rather, this book is something you can pick up, get some information, comfort, and guidance from the narrative or picture, and perhaps read one page that will inspire you for this particular moment in time.

As a member of the Jewish clergy, I am invested as a Cantor functioning as a Rabbi and a healer for my congregation. I have worked for the past 15 years with those who are ill and dying and their families. Like everyone alive, I have experienced loss. Loss of my father during my first year of life, abandonment by my mother before I entered kindergarten, loss of children before they were born, loss of physical capacities due to accidents and illness, and loss of my husband just as we reached our empty nest. It is in those losses I have discovered my greatest gift, and that is an empathy and a calm with those who are experiencing transition and loss in their lives.

In my work with those who are ill and dying and their families, time after time, the five discussions I learned from Dr. Adam Kendall in my late husband's hospital room have been the solace that the families tell me they found the most helpful. I share some of their stories as well as insights and stories of my own to speak to you on those days when all you need is a voice to let you know you are not alone.

Sue Knight Deutsch

A WORD ABOUT CONNECTION:
Part of my story

The sky was grey, a typical English gloomy day, and there were different shades and shapes of clouds moving across the sky. The little seven-year-old girl had been sent to play in the sandbox, with only the loud crows squawking above for company. It was in the early 1960s, and the place was a Christian children's home in the East Anglian countryside of England. The little girl's father had been dead since she was six months old, and her mother had been in a psychiatric unit for two years. The little girl had ended up in this place after being bounced through a few other foster homes. It hadn't always been that way, though. For the first four years of her life, her uncle, the brother with whom her 26-year-old mother had sought refuge when widowed with a baby, had raised the little girl.

The uncle had a beautiful tenor voice. He sang the little girl to sleep at night, songs ranging from Shakespeare's poetry to Jewish folk songs and Cantorial music. Every week on the Sabbath, her uncle took her to the big synagogue; the Orthodox one where the men sat downstairs and the women sat upstairs in the gallery. The splendor of the stained glass windows and the chorus of the voices with the plaintive modes of the music spoke to the little girl of God, that great, loving, powerful presence who was the protector of her people and all mankind. She felt connected to that presence of the Holy One, and that presence never left her, even in those moments when she was physically alone. On that grey, dreary English day, the children of the home were excited for visiting day. Those children who had one or more parents would be collected and taken out, and volunteers of the Big Brother/Sister organization would take out those children who were orphaned. The little girl waited for her mother, who was supposed to have been released from the hospital for the day to visit. When all the children had been collected and it was clear that her mother was not going to show up, the housemother said, "Suzy, it looks like nobody wants you. Go outside and play."

Suzy lay back in the sandbox, staring up at the cloudy sky, and it appeared to her that in the shapes of the clouds, she saw the face of God. More importantly, she felt that God was listening to her and she was connected to God. She spoke to God: "God, I am only little, and except for you I'm all alone. I can't physically protect myself from these people who are hurting me, but if you will please protect me from them and keep me alive, I promise to be the best me I can be and work to bring people closer to you."

The very next day, Suzy was sent with a note pinned to her threadbare coat to ask a local Jewish family who lived down the street for Hebrew lessons. The matriarch of that family took one look at Suzy and saw an emaciated and haunted look very similar to that of the child Holocaust survivors of her native Germany, and she knew that Suzy had been sent to her for a reason.

Though I call myself Sue now, I am Suzy. I now live in California, and I am an invested Cantor in the Conservative movement of Judaism and the spiritual leader of a congregation whose ages range from 70 to 107. No matter what has happened or continues to happen in my life, I have never lost that connection to that powerful force that I believe exists in the universe and always works for the greater good. I alternate between calling this presence "God," "The Universe," "The Mystery," and "Spirit." It has no gender and no name, no body or form other than energy. It is loving and always answers me, even when the answer is silence. I start this book with this Force because it is the energy that I work with when I connect with other people, and it is my hope that you will

11

feel this energy, whether you call it God, Universe, Spirit, Mystery, Intuition or whatever name resonates with you.

This book itself, however, came about for a very different reason: As I sat in a hospital room with my dying husband in front of me and my children around me, I learned something from Dr. Adam Kendall, the palliative care doctor assigned to our case when it became clear that Michael had only weeks to months to live. As it turned out, it would only be two days, and Dr. Kendall unwittingly changed my life, and in the process of transformation that followed, I am in turn paying it forward to others both in my professional and personal life, and now in this book, keeping the promise I made long ago on that dreary day in England.

THE POWER OF THE HAND

Chances are that by reading this, you are holding a book or a digital pad, and you are holding it with two very powerful instruments—your hands. Your hands are functional in performing everyday tasks, but they are so much more than just functional equipment.

Think for a moment about how you use your hands. When someone is crying, you may place your hand on theirs to transmit comfort, or take a tissue in your hand to wipe away their tears. We connect to each other in a myriad of ways by the use of our hands. Now take your hands and rub them vigorously together, and as soon as you stop the motion, hold your hands with your palms facing each other. Can you feel the energy, not only in the surface of the hand, but like a throbbing sensation between the two hands? This energy is something that you can use to heal and to connect to another.

I perform a daily prayer ritual in which I wear a prayer shawl, and at a particular prayer, I take the fringes from my prayer shawl and wrap them around the ring finger of my left hand. The prayer is known as the Shemah, whose first line contains the basic tenet of Judaism that God is One, and it is a prayer that almost every Jew will recognize, even at a soul level. The words come directly from the Torah. In this prayer, I am told to love God with all my heart, might and soul. A few paragraphs later, I switch the fringes to the index finger of my right hand and read a passage where I am instructed to wear those fringes on the corner of my garment and to do the commandments in the Torah. Why switch from the left to the right hand? Rabbi Bernie King told me that the ring finger of the left hand is connected to the heart and the index finger of the right hand is one of action, so when I speak about my love for God, I wind the fringes around my ring finger of the left hand, but transfer them to the finger of action—signifying that loving is not just a feeling but also an action. When you feel love for someone and do nothing to show that love, then that love is not given its full expression. To act with love is to transmit your feeling in a concrete way to bring about change so that the person will feel loved. How you act will depend on the given situation. How do you act to show the person that you love them? Often, your action does not need to be a grandiose display of affection, but rather in the small nuances of a kiss, a smile, or in something practical like giving someone a ride when it is needed.

And so it is with the hand—through our hands we feel, but also we act. Human touch is so important that if we did not have it we would die. Particularly when someone is ill, it makes a difference as to how they are touched. When my late husband Michael was in the hospital dying and had all sorts of medical tubes connected to his body, it was difficult to lie in bed with him and cuddle and comfort him, so I lay on a cot next to his bed, holding his hand, staying connected, feeling and transmitting warmth, comfort and healing. It was the jerking of his hand away from mine that woke me up just before he died. It was my hands that held his face and signaled to him that he was not alone as he took his last breath.

Two days prior to Michael's death, the palliative care doctor, Dr. Kendall, came to discuss putting my husband on hospice. When we had made the decision to do so, he told us that there were some things that we might want to discuss with him before he died. It would allow for closure and it would allow Michael to die in peace. My children, who were going back and forth from the hospital to my house or to their school, would call me and ask, "What were those things again?" I looked down at my hands and I had an idea. "Look at your hand," I said.

On the thumb is "Thank You,"
On the index finger is "Please Forgive Me,"
On the middle finger is "I Forgive You,"
On the ring finger is "I Love You," and
On the little finger is "Goodbye,"

In addition to all that the hand can do by way of touch and action, it also served as a memory tool for some very important concepts of life and death, and for letting go from life into death. Even the concept of letting go is a release of the hand. A baby comes into this world with a clenched fist, but we die with our hands completely open as we let go.

The hand can hurt as well as heal. How you choose to use your hand, either with a gentle touch, a firm touch, a grasp, or a squeeze provides silent communication that goes to a place beyond where words can reach. How someone touches you makes all the difference in how you feel as you are touched.

Take a moment right now to be aware of how you are holding this book. How do your hands feel? Is there any other part of your body that feels tense or stressed? How might touch affect how you feel? If you touched someone else right now, what would you be communicating?

THE FIVE-FINGER MODEL

How do you say goodbye knowing that you will never physically hold this person again? Start with the feeling of what it is like to be the one that must say goodbye. How do you trust that there is something beyond what your five senses can see? Open your heart. Let the trust and faith come into your being. Know that you are held by forces larger than you can conceive of, and in so knowing, trust that the goodbye is simply a transformation of your relationship. You will never really lose your beloved; only your connection will change form. In the final stage, you will recognize and know that it is about to occur. There may be initial shock and then the gradual dawning of realization that there is precious little time to say what you need to say. And here is where your hand comes in—your healing hand that you were born with. Your hand, with its five fingers, its palm that can be cupped to hold, and all those lines written on it that are uniquely yours. Take that eternal hand now with me, and learn how to have the discussions that will ease the journey of both you and your beloved.

Five fingers. On the first is written 'Thank you." Thank you for what you did for me, gave to me, loved me, and supported me. Tell your beloved without thinking so hard—let your heart do the talking. Then stop a while and listen. What does your beloved say or do in response? What gestures do they use? Listen with your ears and also with your being. Gratitude is important. We want to know that we came to this planet for a reason and that our lives had purpose and meaning. Let them know that even if they are no longer here, you will continue on with the strength of the gifts they gave you.

Second finger: "Please forgive me." You may not know of any hurt and pain that you have caused, but just in case, it needs to be voiced. Listen with an open heart.

And if forgiveness is asked for, do your best to let it go and forgive.

Third finger: "I forgive you." No one is perfect, and even though at this moment I may not be able to think of one thing to forgive you for, you may be thinking of something you need forgiveness for that I am unaware of. What if you can't forgive them? What if it can't be resolved in your mind right here and now? Forgiving someone whether they need it or not is removing any and all imagined debts, and is really saying "I acknowledge that you are/were not perfect and I love you unconditionally." Do it for yourself as well as for them. Try to imagine how you might feel if they were gone and you had not forgiven them. Will you regret not expressing forgiveness? Be honest, and be gentle with your honesty.

Fourth finger: "I love you." Let this shine from your eyes as you say it. Let your heart pour forth its loving energy. "I love you." Say it softly, loudly, gently. Say it over and over in as many ways as you can with your breath and the knowledge that the fourth finger is connected to the heart.

Fifth finger: "Goodbye." The fifth finger is the most difficult of all. It means you must release your beloved, even though you may not want to. It is "goodbye" and it will break you open, even as the doorway to the spirit world both opens and shuts. "Goodbye."

This world was changed forever when you entered it and will be forever changed without your physical presence here.

TEACH DEATH FIRST

You make a wish and you blow out the candles. That's how we celebrate birthdays in the West, marking the anniversary of our birth and the continued life journey. To whom are we speaking when we make that wish? And why do we blow the candles out when the light is what we seek? If you ask elderly European Jews when their birthdays are, they often do not know the date. They will tell you that they were born around or between one of the many holidays that mark the passage of time in the Jewish calendar. But ask them when a loved one died, and they will not only be able to tell you the date, but also if it was before sundown (when the Hebrew "day" begins and ends). It is a tradition in Judaism to remember the death of the loved one by lighting a memorial candle on the anniversary of the death. This candle burns for 24 hours and is not blown out. It is said that the candle represents the light of the soul.

Every religious and spiritual practice has a ritual around death. In Jewish tradition, there is a loving practice of ritual purification and preparation of the body for burial. The Chevra Kadisha "Holy Society" is a group of people specially trained to lovingly bathe the body and dress the deceased in white shrouds, the same shrouds as the ones worn at a wedding and on Yom Kippur. During this process, permission and forgiveness is asked of the deceased, prayers are said, and movement around the head is not permitted. The shrouds are tied in such a way as to spell the letters of God's name, and shards of pottery are placed on the eyes and mouth, symbolizing that they are broken and unable to see or speak of God's glory on this earth anymore. Before leaving the preparation room, the members of the society hold the feet of the deceased, make a wish and ask the soul to go on its journey and take the wish with them to the next world.

Why would our tradition forget people's birthdays but remember their death days? It actually makes sense that there is more to celebrate about someone's life when it is over, because it is over and the extent of their legacy and dreams can be measured in terms of that life. In modern times when people often die in hospitals and are whisked away to mortuaries so that the sight of a dead body is unfamiliar to the general population, it also makes sense when teaching children about lifecycle events and rituals to teach death first.

Death has much to teach us about life. Every ending holds a new beginning, so let us start at the end in celebration.

PARKING YOURSELF AT THE DOOR:
Entering a sick room with presence

The first thing to remember is that your intention counts when you enter a hospital room. When you are coming from a place of wanting to connect, all that comes forth will be for the greater good and nothing you say will be wrong.

How do you get to that place? You are already on that journey just by measure of reading this book.

Before you enter the room, it will be helpful to speak to the doctor or nurse caring for your loved one to ask about your loved one's physical condition. In addition to giving you practical information, this serves to remind the doctor that their patient is more than their patient, but also someone's beloved. Sometimes, a doctor will perceive from scientific evaluation that your loved one is unable to hear you and is no longer present in their body. Medical doctors are practitioners of the body, not spiritual practitioners. Trust what your gut tells you. Your soul knows. I believe that a person's spirit does not leave until the body is no longer functioning to contain it, and the body will stop functioning at exactly the right time. If there is an issue of disconnection from life support, be assured that whatever decisions are made are all in the service of the journey of the spirit.

If you are already in the room of the one who is dying, please go outside for the moment. If you are outside already, then we may begin.

- First, pause and breathe out, and with the out-breath, imagine all the sadness, pain and negativity leaving your body on the breath.
- Then, slowly draw your breath inward through the nose, imagining the breath going deep into your belly.

- Expand your rib cage with your breath.
- Then expand the space beneath your collarbones.
- Hold the breath there for a second.
- Then release again, this time through the mouth, and with this outbreath, imagine that all your day-to-day concerns form a bundle that is your practical function in the world, and park that bundle of your everyday self at the door.
- Imagine a thread coming out the top of your head and lifting you up.
- Your shoulders move back and down.
- Take one more breath in, this time breathing in strength and courage.
- Finally, breathe out, and on the outbreath, send strength and courage to every cell in your body.

You may now feel ready to enter the room. You will feel this readiness by a sense of lightness of being and a sense of power. Keep the breathing cycle going until you are fully ready to enter the room with this sense of presence.

When you enter the room, you are entering with the intention to connect with your loved one. In turn, no matter what condition your loved one is in, trust that they can hear you and sense your presence. You will use all your senses to give you information as to how to connect with them. Your eyes will tell you if the person is asleep or awake, what the monitors (if there are any) are saying, who is in the room and what their body language is transmitting. Your ears will hear the sound of the breathing and if it is labored or not, or you will hear silence, or the echo of what may be going on outside. Your sense of touch, particularly through the hands, is what you will use to connect. Make your movements slow and gentle.

Take a seat or bend your body such that you are level with the person in the bed or on the chair. Ask the person for their permission to touch them. If they are conscious, and they agree, or if they are unconscious, place your open left hand on their forehead, with the third and fourth fingers of your hand placed together on the space between your loved one's eyes, similar to placing your hand on the forehead if you were checking for a fever. With your right hand, take their hand, initially squeezing it gently, and then hold it firmly but gently. Bring your mouth close to their ear, in a very gentle voice speak their name, and tell them your name and relationship to them. Softly sing any song or prayer that comes to your mind, especially one that you know will resonate with them. Again speak their name and announce who you are and your relationship to them. Tell them how much you love them and how important they are to you. Speak of all the life lessons and spiritual gifts that they have given you and how meaningful those gifts are to you, and how these will sustain you long after the person is gone, and say thank you. Forgive them in the way that only you know how. Even if you feel there is nothing to forgive, they may feel that there is something left unsaid, they may feel that there is something left unsaid, and it is up to you now to voice that fear and release it. If there is something that you would like to be forgiven for, ask for that forgiveness and tell them that you are certain that they forgive you for whatever you feel it is you need forgiveness for. And if you feel there is nothing to ask for forgiveness for, still ask, just in case there is a wounding they may not have told you that they need to clear.

Thank them again for all they have taught you, given you, contributed to you to make you who you are. What is important here is not what they hear, but what you say and the honesty with which you say it. Love, for-giveness, and gratitude take many forms. If you cannot feel what you might like to feel, it is helpful to think of a place and time that you would like to have had, or did have that feeling. Your words can be direct without being judgmental.

Repeat their name and yours. Then it is time to let them go. Release your hands from theirs, now maintaining the gentle touch in a stroking motion, at the hairline, the top of the head, along the arms and out their hands, all the while telling them that all is well and it is all right for them to walk toward the light. It is all right for them to release and relax and continue on their journey, and that you will continue on yours with the gifts they have given you safely tucked inside your heart.

Sit quietly by the bedside. Take hold of their hand again, enclosing their hand or hands with both of yours. Close your eyes and allow an image to come to your mind. Sing softly or be still, whatever you feel you need to do in that moment. Visualize yourself walking hand-in-hand with your loved one toward a light, then gently let go of the hand with the words "I love you, I have always loved you, I will always love you."

PRESENCE

It was a Sabbath afternoon and I had already conducted synagogue services that morning for two hours. I was leaving the synagogue exhausted and fatigued from having worked hard through Passover and having officiated at the unveiling of Michael's headstone the day before, and then, immediately following, traveling to New York from California for the Cantors Assembly convention. Someone for whom I cared deeply chose that moment to verbally put me down, and, with my defenses down, I allowed myself to feel small and insignificant. I started to leave the building, intending to go home and curl up in a little ball, but on my way out, I was called to the hospital to minister to a family whose loved one was on life support. The man's wife did not want to remove him from life support, but his children wanted to honor the man's wish not to extend his life by artificial means. I walked across the street to the hospital and to the fourth-floor CICU, stood outside for a moment, let a long breath out as I relaxed my shoulders and allowed a long breath in to come. I found the patient's room, "parked my 'self' at the door" and went in. Make no mistake—this action was as important as any I would make in the following hours. It is essential when walking into a hospital room to leave your baggage outside. You need to enter the room totally receptive and prepared to be present for the person who is inside, needing your healing hand.

When I walked to the bedside, it was my hands I first extended to the dying man. I assessed the situation in the room, and, being open and receptive, I could feel the energy present and intuit how to relate to the people who needed my help, my full presence, and my healing energy.

The family told me that the patient in the bed was unaware of what was going on and unable to respond to any conversation. They thought that the machine was keeping his body going, but that mentally he was already gone. I saw a man lying in the bed with tubes in his nose and mouth, who stared at me with a deep blue-eyed gaze. I sensed that he was very much present but physically incapable of normal speech and response. With my right hand, I reached out and grasped his right hand, and I held my face and gaze level with his. "Leonard, I know that you can hear me, but you cannot speak. Your family is here, Ina is over there (motioning my head to the left), and Sally and James are there (motioning to the right). So I am going to ask you some questions that will only require a yes or no answer and I am going to ask you to blink once for no and twice for yes. If you can blink, please do so twice right now."

Leonard slowly and deliberately blinked twice. I heard his family, who were watching closely, suck in their breath, and I knew that they were suddenly aware that they could communicate with their husband and father. It was this communication that would ultimately determine the course of Leonard's treatment and begin the process of letting go and saying goodbye. Within the next two hours, after I worked as the conduit between Leonard and his wife and children, all were in agreement to take Leonard off life support, as was his wish.

Letting go means releasing the hand — not just the physical hand, but also the spiritual hand with which we hold each other and with which we connect. Understanding, believing and trusting that there is a larger, more powerful spiritual hand that always holds us is helpful in aiding the process of letting go. Being present allows this process to unfold.

107ᵗʰ BIRTHDAY:
Questions to engage a conversation

I went to see Juliet for her 107ᵗʰ birthday today. I took her a single rose—the most beautiful and fragrant one I could find in my garden. You see, she can only see shapes due to macular degeneration, and she can only hear when you shout right next to her ear, and she has stopped eating because food has lost its taste. So what do you bring to a 107-year-old whose only acute senses are those of touch, smell and presence? Yourself, and something from nature that smells good, of course.

A reporter asked her what it was like to be 107. "I don't know." What do you think about technology? "I don't know." What surprised you over the last 107 years? "I don't know." What do you think about? "I don't know."

After sitting by Juliet's bedside, laying my hands on her head, singing to her and blessing her, all while the reporter snapped pictures, I asked Juliet about the passage of time in the following way: Does it feel like things happened yesterday or a long time ago? "Oh, everything feels like so long ago." And how does time feel? "Like it goes on and on, just going and going." Do your memories come in pictures or thoughts with words or another form? "Pictures, but all the pictures are jumbled up." (Memories are often out of sequence in reference to time—time is not linear to the spirit, I've found.) Are the pictures in color? "Yes, some of the memories have more faded color, but the really happy and really sad memories have a lot of color."

Does the world feel different now that there are computers instead of shorthand and typing? "Oh yes, my shorthand beats a computer any day, and I am sad when sitting at a computer actually makes you listen less. You have to listen more when you take shorthand."

There is wisdom in the answers, but bringing forth that wisdom happens more in the way the question is asked. This is what I communicated to the reporter by advising her to ask Juliet about feelings rather than thoughts. Particularly with the elderly, whose brains may be deteriorating but their spirit is not, it is the spirit that holds the memory and needs to be accessed through feeling. It is often difficult to phrase a question to access a feeling instead of a thought.

While Juliet was lying in the bed, her age was being treated as an accomplishment in itself, and yet there was much value in the life still there other than just being there. As she was listening to me talk to Juliet and heard my accent, the reporter suddenly remembered me from the funeral she had attended that I had conducted the month before, where the daughter of the deceased was the editor of the newspaper she works for. She had asked the daughter for the poem I had used at the funeral, but the daughter didn't know and didn't connect me with the reporter. It was then the reporter asked me about her own spiritual life and, after a few minutes of listening and responding, I turned to Juliet, and told her that although she may think she is lying in the bed doing nothing, she had in fact made a difference by bringing all the different people together in the room to celebrate her life, who in themselves made a connection. I said, "When you open your eyes in the morning, Juliet, never think that you are an inanimate object with no use—even the caregivers around you feel happy when the things they do for you make you feel comfortable. You never know whom you will touch merely by your presence."

It is simple, really. The reporter, believing in coincidences, felt that she had stumbled on a series of coincidences and that I had made them spiritual for her. As I do not believe in coincidence, I believe that in that room I had been a vehicle for the spiritual connection between the living, and I know that my presence made a difference. This capacity is available to every human being who is open to that connection.

MICHAEL'S WISH AND
THE ETIQUETTE OF ILLNESS

I would be remiss if I did not include in this book a wish that my husband Michael made before he died. An industrial and manufacturing engineer, Michael couldn't spell, and his stellar writing accomplishments were usually technical scratches and fascinating inventions. I have less than a page of notes he made, and an armful of memories of the feelings he described to me.

When Michael was diagnosed with colon cancer, it was already at stage IV and was a rare, quickly growing form of cancer that had metastasized to his spine, ribs and pelvis. He died five months and one week after his diagnosis, and during every day of that time, he fought to live. One of the things he wanted to do was to write and publish a book called "The Etiquette of Illness." In it, he wanted to detail how to respond to someone who has just shared with you that they are gravely ill. He found it upsetting to tell someone he had cancer and then to be regaled with tales from that person about someone they knew or were related to who had cancer and what happened to them and what treatment they tried. Michael had not asked for their advice. He didn't want to know about anyone else's story. He was basically telling them, hey, I could be dying, I am in pain, and I'm afraid. What he wanted was an acknowledgement and, if possible, empathy.

Although he understood that people meant well and that they were intending to help, in actuality what they were doing was taking the focus off Michael and putting the focus on themselves or someone else. He also understood that people were sometimes uncomfortable and did not know what to say or how to help.

Some pointers:

- Even if you think your advice is good, wait until you are asked for it.
- Those who are ill want and need empathy, not sympathy. In her talk, "The Power of Empathy," Brené Brown notes the difference between empathy and sympathy as follows:
  - Empathy is connection, looking at something from the perspective of the other person, withholding judgment, recognizing the emotion in another person and identifying with it in yourself. "I don't know what to say, I'm glad you told me," or "you are not alone," are good starting points.
  - Sympathy is disconnection; it does not acknowledge the feelings of the other person and diminishes or distracts from the feeling. Avoid statements such as: "That sucks! At least you still have your hair."
  - Your response itself will not make them feel better; what will make them feel better is when your response makes an emotional connection.
- Do not deny or diminish their pain or fear.
- If you are willing to help, be specific about how you can help (rides, cooking, listening, massage, etc).
- If you say, "call me if there's anything you need," generally, they won't, but if they do, be prepared to step up!

When someone shares with you that they are ill and you don't know what to say, be the listener. Even if you do know what to say, be the listener. Remember to breathe out and keep your breathing steady and calm, so that you can be present, mindful, and send a non-verbal message to transmit that calm presence to the person who is ill. Sometimes, the best response is reaching out your hand and holding theirs, or giving a gentle hug with no words at all.

CHICKEN SOUP

Ah, the power of prayer: When I went to visit a congregant in the hospital, I arrived to her screaming. She was afraid of having medication that had to be injected into her belly. As I arrived, I asked the nurses if I could pray with her to calm her down. As the woman locked her gaze with mine while I held her hands, I sang the Shemah, one of the most-known Hebrew prayers, and she responded in kind, not even flinching as the needle went into her belly. As she had been refusing food for three days, I told her that the next prayer might work better if she took a spoonful of soup in between each word, and then proceeded to feed her while singing. Prayer can be chicken soup for the body and soul indeed.

THANK YOU

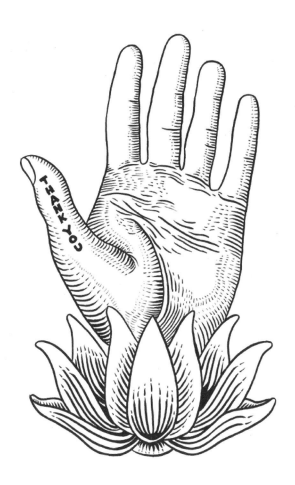

OF COURSE! WEREN'T WE ALL TAUGHT TO SAY THANK YOU?

It would seem to be so easy, right? Weren't we all taught to say "please" and "thank you"? It is so common to hear someone ask a child who makes no verbal response after they have been given something, "What do you say?" or "What are the magic words?" For some of us, it would seem to be automatic, rote even, when someone gives you something, to say "thank you." Yet, how often have you sat in a restaurant and observed people who are being waited on and noticed that many people do not say "thank you" to the waiter? It is a matter of politeness, of course.

Those two words, "thank you," can go beyond politeness when expressing gratitude. Feeling grateful and expressing gratitude are different. One is a feeling and one an action. How do you express your gratitude beyond the words of "thank you"? What if those words don't express the magnitude of your deep gratitude? Here is where you need to describe a situation where you felt gratitude for what your loved one gave you or taught you or did for you. Then describe how it made you feel, how it affected your life, and then how grateful you are for that situation.

What if you don't feel gratitude for the person or anything they did? What if they hurt you in the past? How did that hurt change you? Did you learn anything from it that changed how you are in the world? Perhaps you can turn it into a positive for yourself and thank them for teaching you, even if it is a lesson you would rather not have learned. The point is, our elders were correct: "Thank you" are magic words, especially when expressed so that the person saying them validates an experience and that the person hearing them feels validated.

HOW DO YOU SAY THANK YOU?

Saying "thank you" serves a dual function: For the person doing the thanking to express gratitude, and to let the person they are thanking know that they are appreciated and their life has meaning. The end of someone's life is not the sum total of their existence. Life consists of many ordinary moments that become extraordinary by virtue of connection.

- What are the ordinary moments in your loved one's life that stand out now as an extraordinary, beautiful memory?
    - Have you described them and said "thank you"?
- What has your loved one done for you or said to you that you are grateful for?
    - Have you said "thank you" for what you are grateful for?
- What has your loved one done for others, said to others, and achieved in life that you admire and are grateful for their example?
    - Have you told them about these things and said "thank you" for them?
- How has your loved one made you feel, in good times and in bad?
    - Have you described those feelings and said "thank you" for them?
- Has your loved one disappointed you?
    - Have you told them that you wish it had been better, and you thank them anyway in spite of or maybe because of that?

- What did your loved one not do that you wanted them to do? Did you learn from it? Can you take that feeling you wish you could have felt and pay forward that good wish for them?

- Has your loved one inspired you and supported you?
    - Have you told them, explained how they did so, and thanked them for their inspiration and support?

PHOTOGRAPHS:
A visual of a meaningful life

It is difficult to keep up a running conversation with someone who is ill and who needs to rest. There may be many hours when you feel that you have said all you can say and you sit in silence wanting to say more, but not knowing what to say. That is where old photographs and current photographs can offer a way of reminding your loved one about the times in their life that were meaningful. Photographs are excellent prompters of memory and conversation.

When Michael was in the hospital, I took all our albums and photographs to his room and went through many of them, asking:

> Remember when..........?
>
> How did you feel about........?
>
> Whatever happened to.........?
>
> Look what you did for her/him!
>
> Many other questions specific to the photograph and the story it told.

This had the effect of giving him the assurance that his life had been made up of many meaningful moments and that there was a physical record of his smile, his humor, and his values.

Michael's niece got married in Israel while he was sick, and we could not attend the wedding because of his illness. I will not forget his smile when his brother brought in the video of the wedding, nor the comment that he remembered holding her on his shoulder when she was a baby and comforting her. Michael loved babies and had a knack for soothing a crying baby—even ones that he had never encountered before.

What can you see in a photograph or a video that prompts a memory of your loved one's special qualities and legacy that you can share?

TEA AND DAFFODILS

Although the odds of Michael's diagnosis made survival slim, Michael's oncologist told him that chemotherapy would ease his pain by reducing the cancer, so Michael chose to have chemotherapy. He also hoped that he would beat the odds. Every time we drove to the oncology clinic for Michael to have chemotherapy—which was for six hours a day for four consecutive days every other week—I packed snacks, tea, his reading materials, and games for him. Too weak to carry anything, and walking either with a cane or a walker to get to the car by himself, I carried his things and had him lean on me as he slowly got into the car. Later, as he deteriorated, I lifted a wheelchair as well. Michael was 55 years old; I was 53. It really bothered him to lose his independence, but even more so, he felt that he was a burden on me, although I never felt him to be so. I was working, and arranged my schedule so that I could be available to take him to and from chemotherapy and sit with him for some of the time he was undergoing the therapy. Sometimes, I had to leave him to go and teach a class, and that is what felt like a burden—carrying on my "normal" life when I really wanted to care for him and myself and not worry about anything else. I did what I knew how to do, and it did not occur to me to ask for help unless the chemotherapy schedule changed and I had to ask a friend to give him a ride because I couldn't get back in time.

When I left Michael to go to work, I knew that he had plenty of company with the other patients who were also undergoing treatment and who would sometimes play chess with him, joking with each other about "chemo brain" making checkmate a strong possibility. We became a sort of family, knowing each other's diagnoses and meeting each other's family members.

On public holidays, the oncology clinic was closed, so Michael would take his treatments at the hospital. One time when we went to the hospital, it was daffodil season and the American Cancer Society volunteers were sitting in the lobby giving out daffodils to the cancer patients as we left. They gave him a choice of an orange or a clear vase. It was the school holidays and our daughter Alexandra was with us. Michael asked her to choose the vase. She chose the orange one. Daffodils filled our house daily from that point on. During the last week of his life, a friend brought daffodils to the hospital, and told him not to think he had slept for a long time if he woke up and found the closed buds completely open, because daffodils bloom very quickly. Michael told me later that while contemplating his life, he would stare at them for a long time and could see them moving as they opened.

I was going back and forth to the hospital for the first few days that Michael was there during the last week of his life. Every day, I would bring his thermos from home with the strong Yorkshire tea that he liked, and some special food treat. I was quite frazzled between trying to keep up my job and meet the bills and be with Michael as much as I could. One day, I brought his tea, and Michael sighed heavily, a sort of protest sigh, and said, "Oh, you should not be having to go through this, Sue!"

"Through what?" I asked, incredulous that he was thinking of me while he was dying. "Through bringing me tea, and all the financial stuff, and through worrying about me!" he said. I looked at him like he had lost his mind. It dawned on me then that he felt bad that I was having a hard time and felt powerless to do anything about it. He also felt that I was being cheated out of a mid-life relationship with him, and worried that I would be left alone without him. "Don't be ridiculous!" I said.

"I love you and I wish I could do more for you. I would not want to be deprived of the ability to help you."

"Thank you, Sue. Thank you for everything you have ever done for me, but most of all, thank you for loving me and making me feel loved, for helping me to maintain my dignity and feel safe even though I feel helpless." He pursed his lips in frustration even as he expressed his gratitude. To this day, the orange vase sits in my living room, always full of yellow flowers, and when it is daffodil season, I go out and cut them from my garden where I planted them in his honor after Michael died. When I arrange the daffodils in the little vase, I hear his voice whispering "thank you" in the spring breeze, and I pour myself a cup of tea.

ANCIENT COMFORT

Passover had been quite a week, with joy, celebration, loss, and mourning. When an old man put his head on my shoulder and sobbed for his son who had just died, I felt my grandmother weeping for my young father, and from deep inside my heart she reached out to comfort him. We stand on the shoulders and in the presence of those who came before us.

Who is your tribe? What ancient teachings and memories do you hold that you can pass on? You are a link in that chain. How will your future generations look back to you in times of joy and need and loss, and what will they thank you for?

AN ESALEN DAY:
Appreciating the ordinary moments

Esalen is like a spiritual oasis for me. Perched atop the cliffs in Big Sur, California, it is an alternative education institute, and the place I go to regroup, recharge, reconnect with earth and spirit, and to learn. In 1983, Michael and I were supposed to go to take a workshop together at Esalen, but the roads were closed due to a storm, and by the time they were clear, I was about ready to give birth to our second child, so we waited, taking a credit on our deposit. By 1986, we still hadn't gone, and I urged Michael to go and take a workshop while I stayed home with our children. Michael took a workshop with George Leonard and brought me back an Esalen t-shirt and tales of wonder at this place called Esalen, that for some reason we never went to together, nor did he ever go back.

It took me over a year to break open after Michael died. One night, after someone I loved really hurt my feelings, I found myself curled up on the floor in a fetal position, crying hysterically, and in those moments where I caught my breath through the shuddering and tears, I realized that it was not the words of the person that were causing me so much pain—it was the grief that I had not yet expressed. I was in so much pain that it was difficult for me to stand in an upright position, and yet I still had to suck it up and somehow sing and speak on my pulpit that very evening. My congregation asked me if I was okay as I kept clutching my stomach, and I told them I had reflux. The next morning, I went on my usual run, and I knew that I had to get away and give myself the space to come to terms with my new life. But where should I go? I asked aloud. Just then, I looked down at my chest and across the t-shirt I had thrown on that morning was the word "Esalen." For me, it was a sign.

Although because of my work schedule I could not leave town for five weeks, I went on the internet to see if Esalen was still in existence, and found that not only was it still there, but the very week I could get away there was a workshop entitled, "Water in the desert: Faith, Hope and Awe in a time of Loss" taught by Dr. Maria Sirois. That stay at Esalen and meeting Dr. Sirois was to be the pivot point in my transformation, opening me up to the life I have now. What follows is one of my many gratitude-learning experiences at Esalen.

Completely submerged and floating in a mineral bath at Esalen, I felt the healing waters wash over me and heard the sound of my own heart beating as the water enveloped my body. Weightless, buoyed by the water, every muscle responded with gratitude. As I left the baths, relaxed, warm and smiling with my towel in hand, I walked up the dirt path to the big wooden receptacle where the used towels were thrown to be washed. It was time to empty it, and one of the work scholars was gathering up the towels for the laundry. I hesitated before throwing the towel, and she said, "Just toss it in with the others." Knowing that I use two towels a day at the baths, as do others, I said, "That's an endless task you have there!" She smiled at me and said, "Yes, it's a thankless job."

"Are you kidding?" I asked. "I so appreciate it when I come down to the baths and there are always fresh towels, beautifully folded and kept warm for me to use. I have never had to ask for one because they are always there. Not only that, but I have a choice of navy, maroon, green or brown! Thank you; thank you so much for doing what you do to make that happen! What an amazing job you have!"

She beamed at me as I walked away, and said, "Have an Esalen day!"

"I will," I called back.

"I said, 'Esalen,' which is better than 'Excellent'!" she exclaimed.

Earlier that day, I had eaten meals made from the produce I had seen picked that morning as I walked through the gardens and thanked the workers knee-deep in lettuce. After every meal, I went into the kitchen and thanked the people who lovingly prepared the meal, and always received a smile in return and often the words "Have an Esalen day," as I walked away.

There is no such thing as a thankless job if someone says "thank you." And here's the rub—even in a situation that seems like it has nothing to redeem itself, or in a person who you may find difficult to find the good, sometimes what they didn't do is something you can be thankful for when you look at it as a gratitude moment. Every day can be an Esalen day if we choose to find its meaning.

FORGIVE ME

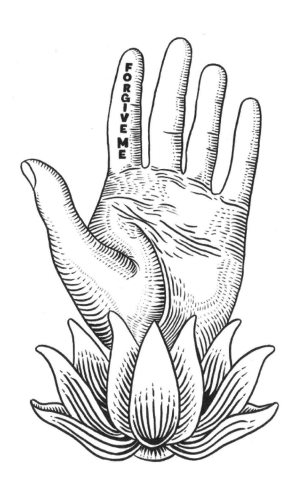

Sue Knight Deutsch

SAYING SORRY AND ASKING FOR FORGIVENESS

When the film "Love Story" came out, I was 15 years old, and it was just months before my foster parents, with whom I had lived for seven years, would send me back to live with my birth mother permanently. I was then old enough to take care of my birth mother, who had spent years in and out of psychiatric institutions. My relationship with my birth mother was complicated, to say the least. When I went to the theatre alone to watch the movie and heard the line, "Love means never having to say you're sorry," I didn't believe it.

Saying that you are sorry and asking for forgiveness are two different things, yet one needs to happen for the other to occur. The person asking for forgiveness needs to acknowledge the wrong that was perpetrated or felt to be perpetrated, express remorse, and to take ownership and accountability for whatever they feel they need forgiveness for. They need to be open to forgiveness, and also to understand that forgiveness may not happen. It is in the asking that healing can occur.

Even if you feel that you have not done or said anything wrong to the person who is ill, there may be a wounding that they have not expressed to you. By asking for forgiveness for anything you may have done to hurt them, it can either bring up a hurt that will find resolution, or, simply by asking, the person will know that you want to make sure that nothing between you goes unsaid. They can then choose to forgive you without having to voice the hurt, only the absolution.

One thing you cannot do: You cannot ask another person to forgive you for something you did or said to someone else. Forgiveness needs to come from the person who was wronged.

HOW DO YOU ASK FOR FORGIVENESS?

It is difficult to ask for forgiveness, because then you have to admit wrong-doing. The anonymity of the confession box makes it easier to admit wrong-doing than to come face-to-face with the person you have wronged. You will likely meet with the resistance of your ego, or the guilt and shame of your transgression. You will make yourself vulnerable. Your loved one is also in a vulnerable place. Asking for forgiveness takes courage. What if you are not forgiven? Will that feel like rejection?

Breathe out. Allow a clear deep breath to come in. Look at your index finger, the finger of action, the finger that can be pointed in accusation, the finger that can beckon someone to come closer. Choose to beckon your connection.

Are you asking for forgiveness for a judgment you made? Something you said or did? Being thoughtless, or hurtful, or absent?

What are you getting when you are asking for forgiveness?

- You are getting the opportunity to give your loved one the opportunity to wipe the slate clean.
- If your loved one should pass away, you will not suffer the regret of something left unsaid or undone.
- You are getting the opportunity to heal a relationship, receive closure and the calm that comes with letting go of negative emotion.

What if they are not able to forgive you because they are incapacitated?

- Tell them that you know deep in your heart that if they were able to speak, that they are generous of

spirit and you are certain that by expressing your remorse and being accountable, they would forgive you.
Believe this as you say it.

What if your loved one will not forgive you?

- Recognize that this will feel like rejection, and that as
  your intention is truly to express remorse, then it is
  your loved one's issue, and no longer your burden to
  carry.
- Recognize that sometimes forgiveness will not happen, and you are worthy anyway.

What are you giving when you are asking for forgiveness?

- You are empowering your loved one to do something
  generous for you, and also allowing them to feel less
  vulnerable.
- You are giving your loved one the assurance that a
  future in which they may not be present will preserve
  a memory and create a legacy of functional connected
  relationships.

Forgiveness will set you and your loved one free,
no longer holding on to negative emotions or bitterness
that held you in their grip. It is not the forgiveness itself
that counts as much as the very real vulnerability and
courage it takes to accept wrong-doing and rectify it that,
in the end, will set you and your loved one free.

SILLY OLD WOMAN

Everything went wrong that day. All my plans fell through. I woke up feeling terrible for something I had said to a family member, fearing that it may cause my family to fall apart and lead to not having the close-knit family I always wanted.

And then it happened: A monumental conversation occurred that was over fifty years in the making. Having grown up in foster homes after just a few short years of living with my birth mother who has bipolar disorder, I had always been told that as her only child I was responsible for her well-being. She lives in a nursing home in England, and I live in California. I call her every day, and often she is not lucid. On that particular day, she was suffering with a broken foot. During my daily call, I am often doing other things while I speak to her, but that day I needed a break. I poured myself a cup of tea, calmed myself with some deep breathing, sat down in an easy chair, and put my feet up to relax before I dialed my mother. The moment came that she and I had needed for years. My mother was lucid and kept calling herself a silly old woman.

"You're old, but you are not silly," I said.

"Oh, but Sue, I left you alone with strange families. They weren't my family. I wasn't a mother to you. I could have been a better mother to you, but I didn't try hard enough," she wailed.

"You did the best you could given who you were. You needed to take care of yourself," I said.

"But you needed me, and I wasn't there for you. I didn't give you anything!" she said.

"Here's what you gave me, Mother. You gave me an excellent vocabulary and turn of phrase. You taught me the importance of eating healthy food and exercising and using natural therapies. You took me to a makeup school to show me how to apply makeup properly so I could make the best of my appearance. You gave me an interest in astrology and mystery and taught me that there is a God. You showed me vulnerability," I told her.

"My parents raised me to be silly. I was no good to anyone but your father. I didn't give to anyone but him," she said.

"You gave me life and a sense of values, Mother. I forgive you for not being there for me," I said.

Still my mother persisted, "I'm a silly old woman!"

"When that thought comes to you as you are lying there with your broken foot, remind yourself that you are Sue's mother and Sue loves you."

I hoped I was getting through to her, when she countered with, "I've done nothing. I have nothing."

"You gave birth to me, and you have me, three grandchildren and three great-grandchildren. We have your DNA. There is a reason for your being. Thank you for what you have given. I forgive you," I said.

"Oh Sue, I miss you. I love you, and am so grateful that you forgive me. It is what I needed to hear," my mother said, as she let out a long sigh. It had been a long and painful journey to get to the point of forgiving my mother. I wanted to forgive her, yet it was so difficult to do, and I was not sure if I would ever get the opportunity.

Forgiving my mother could only happen in the face of her accountability and remorse. Instead of being annoyed with her, I had to let go and let her know what she had given in order to find my own peace in acknowledging her gift. Then forgiveness followed on the wings of gratitude.

Think of a time when this has happened in your own life. When someone has hurt you deeply and then needs your forgiveness, how do you forgive?

The first step is to be open to forgiving, and to understand that forgiveness may not happen.

I FORGIVE YOU

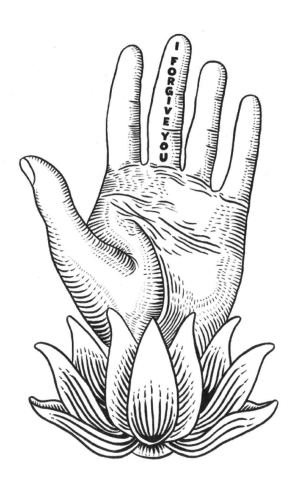

HOW TO FORGIVE

I am fortunate to work with many loving families who, more often than not when I ask them to forgive their loved one, will respond, "I have nothing to forgive them for! They didn't do anything wrong!" Nevertheless, the person who is ill may believe that they have said or done something they need forgiveness for, and your forgiveness will relieve them of this burden. Do not dismiss this need.

What if they have done something that you cannot forgive them for? Or what if they have no remorse and no accountability for what they did or said? Ask yourself: Will forgiving them set me free? Will not forgiving them keep me held in the grip of resentment and bitterness? Sometimes forgiveness does not happen. Asking yourself the question may be enough to let go of the pain and spare you from any self-recrimination after the person has gone.

Although the middle finger is often associated with a rude gesture, in some yogic traditions, the middle finger represents peace and purity. By saying "I forgive you," you are giving your loved one the peace of absolution as well as the purity of having the slate wiped clean for them.

How do you begin the conversation with someone you don't feel has wronged you, especially if your loved one is incapacitated?

- Start by saying that you cannot think of one thing that they have done wrong or would need forgiveness for.
- Acknowledge that no one is perfect, and that just in case they may think there is something they need forgiving for, you bear no grudge or any memory of anything left unsaid or unforgiven. This will allow them to let go and be at peace.

When I do the Viddui (Hebrew for "Confessional," sometimes referred to as Jewish Last Rites) with someone in a hospital room, the text asks God to forgive the person for all those times they could have done better. Perhaps telling your loved one that you know they did the best they could will allow them to make peace with you on some level, and what an enormous gift that is!

FORGIVENESS

As I thought about my daughter's wedding and my excitement grew, I thought back to my own wedding over 35 years ago, walking down the aisle alone with none of my mothers or surrogate fathers attending, and for the first time, instead of feeling like their absence was my loss, I felt incredibly sad for them at how much pleasure and pride they lost by choosing not to be there for me. Forgotten and abandoned children never forget, but they can choose to behave differently and find the compassion to forgive. I am grateful to my daughter and son-in-law for giving me joy beyond measure and healing old wounds.

GERMANY: Addressing the unforgivable

My last foster father, Eli Fachler, was born in Berlin in 1923. Shortly after his fifteenth birthday, he witnessed Kristallnacht (Night of the Broken Glass, also known as the November Pogrom, which is often considered the event that propelled the Holocaust into the killing machine it became) on November 9-10, 1938 from the window of his home with his mother and sister. He watched as the Nazis broke all the windows and desecrated the synagogue across the courtyard. His parents managed to get him and then his little sister out of Germany on the Kindertransport to the safety of England and Scotland. The rest of his family perished in the Holocaust. He never spoke very much about it to me while I was growing up, but in his later years, when he was invited by Germany to revisit his old home, he went, and I started to hear him speak more about it.

My first trip to Germany was in 2012 on a mission with my clergy colleagues of the Cantors Assembly. It was a spectacular mission. We sang in the Berliner Dom, Berlin's huge cathedral, with the Prime Minister of Germany in attendance, as well as many other venues in Berlin and Munich, and we held a service at the Dachau extermination camp. Throughout the mission, despite the intent to bring the beautiful German Jewish music and traditions back to the place where they originated, I felt a heaviness in my heart. When I left Germany that year, I felt the heaviness lift only when the plane took off for Israel, yet still, I was unable to talk about it very much upon my return to the United States. While in Germany, I was interviewed and filmed for the documentary "Prisoners of Hope," where I shared some of my Eli's history and how I felt about it. In the summer of 2013, Eli was invited to speak in his old synagogue in Berlin-Mitte, which was being rededicated on the 75th anniversary of

Kristallnacht. Mike Lam, the producer of "Prisoners of Hope," returned to film this historic event, and I also went, joining 26 other members of my foster family from all over the world, all of them blood relatives of Eli, to watch with pride as this 90-year-old man was honored in the presence of German and other international dignitaries, the Chief Rabbi of Israel, the Chief Rabbi of Russia, and a huge crowd. Security was tight, the event was televised on German television, and I was acutely aware as I watched this gentle man who had raised me speak in his native German tongue about the events of that night, that I was standing in an historic moment in time.

There is so much that I recall about the second trip to Germany that gives me true hope. The heaviness of the previous year was not there, and I am certain it is because of Eli Fachler, and the way in which he behaved and spoke during that week. The very first day he arrived from Israel, I walked from my hotel to see him and meet with the film crew who was going to film him. As it turned out, the film crew got stuck in traffic, and I got to spend some precious time alone with him before things became hectic. I sat with him in a small, dimly lit room in the heart of Berlin-Mitte, just a short walk from the synagogue he had seen smashed 75 years ago. He described for me the events of that night, as he would do over the next few days to everyone from family and schoolchildren to dignitaries. I had so many questions, and one of them was, "How can you forgive? How can you even be here after what they did?" He told me that he grew up in Germany before the war, that he loved the country, and that he had to acknowledge that there would always be evil in the world, but it is up to us to do good so that evil cannot thrive. He told me that he still loves Germany and that his memories sustained him and gave him hope for the future. He pointed out that the current generation of Germans is working to make sure that history is not forgotten and that a way forward is being forged.

The morning after that precious alone-time I had with Eli, I watched and listened as he spoke in German to a new generation of German Jewish schoolchildren. The film crew was filming, and the producer asked him how he felt. Eli raised his hands to the sky, looked up, and said, "Gratitude to God."

Forgiveness may not be ours to grant for another's transgressions. My foster father didn't forgive or forget. He pragmatically spoke of a way forward, knowing that holding a grudge only poisons the present moment. When considering the Holocaust, the emotions and writing about it are vast. When I sat in the room of the synagogue that had once been part of his old house, listened to him describe the events but not consider himself a survivor as he does those who went through the concentration camps, I wondered: Are we responsible for what our forefathers did? We can never restore or expiate the wrong, but we can acknowledge it and vow to do better. Accept responsibility for what has happened, feel remorse, and try to repair. Is that forgiveness? Does forgiveness mean absolution? Even if you cannot forgive the unforgivable, you can find a way to move forward so that the wrong that was perpetrated does not happen again and the people wronged and the wrong that has been done can be acknowledged. The cry of "never forget" does not mean "never forgive." It means, "Let us do better, repair this world, and make it a peaceful place, and let this not ever happen again."

I LOVE YOU

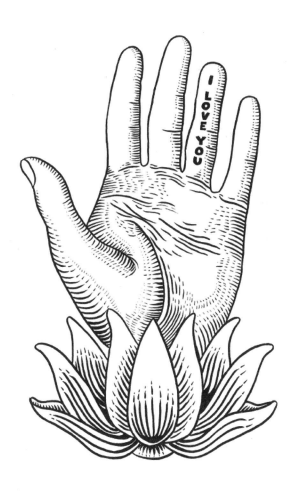

HOW DO I LOVE YOU?

I cannot count the number of times I have made the suggestion to families to say "I love you" to their loved one, and they chuckle. "Well, that's easy!" they say. "I say it every day." Even so, it is more important when someone is ill to not only to hear the words "I love you," but also to be told in what ways you love them. What is it about them that you love? What qualities do they possess that you will miss if they were no longer here? Do they feel loved? Have you shown them that you love them as well as said the words?

What if you don't love the person, but because they are somehow related to you, you feel you ought to say you love them when you don't? I am not suggesting that you be dishonest. Consider: Can you remember a time when you did love them? Is it possible to bring that memory forward and say it to the memory of who they were, using the past tense "I loved you"?

Sometimes, when I am alone in the room with someone who is ill or dying and they have no family, I tell them "You are loved." I can say that in all honesty because I believe that we are all loved by the Divine.

ALLOWING THE SICK TO HEAL
THE CAREGIVER

Just when I think I am useless, that there is nothing I can do for a person who loves and cares for me, who has perhaps been my solace and who I think I have nothing to offer, there comes a crack in the armor. A moment when they show me what it is they need and deep in my solar plexus I know how to respond. It is thus with those who are dying. Even if our relationship to them has been one where one is giving more than receiving, now is your time to step into the reverse role and allow them to heal.

HOW DO I SAY I LOVE YOU WHEN I AM SCARED BY THE WAY YOU LOOK?

Seeing someone who is very ill, especially in a hospital bed with medical tubes in them, can be upsetting, especially when that person is your loved one. Their skin may be a color you are not used to seeing in them, and there may be incisions, rashes, scabs or mottling that is unfamiliar and may make you squeamish. How do you say "I love you" when the person in front of you does not look like the person you know and love?

- Remember that the body is a receptacle that holds the person's essence, their soul and their personality.
- Close your eyes and allow an image to come to your mind of when the person was healthy and happy.
- How did this person being in the world affect you?
- What aspects of their personality made you laugh?
- Focus on the image of who they were before they ended up sick in the bed.

You are connecting to and accessing the feeling of a time when your loved one was healthy and that will allow you to go beyond the image of the body before you and access the person within, whose basic nature has not changed, although the body may be causing them suffering. It is my hope that you can then say, "I love you."

THE HAND RELEASES

Do not fear that goodbye is disconnection. Love simply transforms to another state of being. The connection of spirit will always be there. When it is time to open the hand, you may release and let go of the earthly connection. You will know when you have thanked, forgiven, and loved, and you can trust that the connection will never be lost; even in the darkest, silent moments, it will make its presence known with the touch of a hand.

FAMILIAL DYSAUTONOMIA:
Loving life as it is, and allowing the sick to heal us

Did you know that there is a genetic disease called Familial Dysautonomia that is almost exclusive to Ashkenazi Jews? Most of its victims die before the age of 30 after a great deal of suffering. I was tested for the rare genetic disorder Tay-Sachs disease, which is known to be carried by Ashkenazi Jews, and always counsel couples to get that testing, but I had never heard of FD.

I learned about it from a 93-year-old man I went to visit in CICU whose daughter had died from the disease twenty years ago. He himself was struggling with a medical decision and asked for my help in making the choice. As I held his hands, we spoke for almost an hour, me asking questions, him pouring out the answers already inside him. I watched the heart rate monitor go down from 98 to 72, and when I left the room, he had made his decision.

One of the things he said was that his life no longer had value. "And what do you think your daughter's story did for me today and maybe others I may meet in the future?" I asked. Even on dialysis, with pneumonia and a failing heart, as I reached out to this man, he extended a gift with a value that cannot be measured. If we listen carefully to the stories of those who are ill, not only may we heal them, but also we allow the sick to heal us. Stories have the power to heal.

ANGELS: A tent of love

Where would I be without my angels? It was a busy Passover and I was tired, leaving the synagogue after a long few days, and as I was on my way out of the door, Charlotte stopped me and asked me if I thought there was such a thing as angels. "Of course!" I said, suddenly invigorated. "Why do you ask?" She proceeded to tell me that she believed in them and that some people chided her, telling her Judaism doesn't hold with angels. On the contrary, Judaism speaks of angels, as do many faiths, although they may call them by different names.

When I was a little girl, I was afraid of the dark and needed a nightlight just to feel safe. But then, the nightlight itself would cast shadows on the wall, and I would be afraid of the shadows. My uncle taught me a prayer which is in the standard daily prayer book: "In the name of Adonai, the God of Israel, may Michael be on my right, may Gabriel be on my left, may Uriel be before me, and may Raphael be behind me, and above my head Shechinah, the (female) Presence of God." As I whispered this prayer three times to myself every night, I would feel each angel take their place around me at God's command, with God hovering above my bed, forming a tent of protection during the night. I stopped saying that particular prayer as I became "grown up," but I never forgot it, and my angels never forgot me. Some people call them guides or spirits. As adult life took over and the darkness became real even in the daytime, I learned to pay attention to the shadows and remember that they were cast by light.

I seek guidance daily from my higher power, believing that there is one Source and that all power originates from that Source. I ask for guidance in a variety of ways—in prayer and meditation, in dreams, in opening a book and studying the page that I opened to, and sometimes I pick an angel card, always trusting that deep inside me I already have the answer. My angels are there simply to show me what I already know.

I AM LEAVING YOU BEHIND:
What the dying might feel

I am leaving you behind! How can I leave you behind when you have been my heart's delight? I am not worried about where I am going, but I do worry how you will manage without me. And I worry that you will manage without me and I will be forgotten. Did I love you enough? Was I kind to you? Did I leave you with the tools you need to go on and to thrive? What can I do now as I am failing? I want you to be strong. I want to spare you from the pain of my loss and I want to spare you from the pain of the bad memories as well as the good. I want you to know that there is nothing you have ever done to disappoint me. I am afraid, so afraid, both for me and for you. Assure your loved one while holding their hands that you will always carry them in your heart, and that you will thrive because of the gifts they gave you. Love is eternal and they will not be forgotten.

GOODBYE

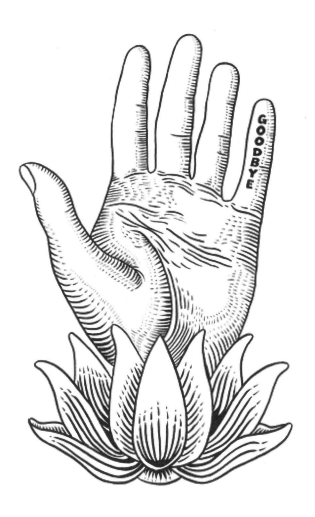

HOW TO LET GO — SAYING GOODBYE

It is never easy to let go of someone you love, either for the person who is dying or for those left behind. Sometimes, the word "goodbye" is impossible to utter. One overarching circumstance I have witnessed in my families who are in the process of letting go is that the person who is dying needs permission from the one they are leaving behind in order to relax into the transition. It can make it even harder for the one left behind, because it is they that will be experiencing the emotional loss in a more catastrophic way than the person dying. The person dying knows this. It doesn't matter if there is a huge amount of love present or not. What matters is that what is meaningful to each party has been said. What matters is what will remain after the person has gone.

It is an act of love to let a person go. It is this love that will propel you to be able to make that sacrifice so that your loved one does not suffer. It is often easier to release for those who believe that the soul continues on its journey after death, but that does not necessarily mean that one has to believe in the Divine in order to let go. Sometimes, not wanting our loved ones to suffer pain is enough to allow us to let them go. Usually, it is the realization that all that can be done has been done, and all that needs to be said has been said. Repeat thank you, all is forgiven, and the admonition that they will not be forgotten before giving them permission by assuring them that you will be all right. Allow them to release or walk toward the light, letting them know that the path is clear, and assure them that you will follow them on a similar journey as you walk to the next stage of your life, carrying them and their legacy with you safely tucked inside your heart.

I have been asked on more than one occasion to provide a script for someone who cannot find the words or language to help someone let go. It is helpful to know the circumstances of the person's illness, and what connections the person has in order to speak directly to the things they may be holding on to. Here is a script I suggested for a healer who wanted to help a client who was dying and who had no family and whose only friends were colleagues. I substitute the name Dee:

"Dee, you are so loved. (Loved one's name) and (loved one's name) are here, loving you, and they will continue to love you as they carry you tucked in their hearts, as will I. Thank you for all you have given to all of us. Your life has made a difference in the lives of others. (Name) and (name) and I want you to know that all is well, and nothing has been left unsaid. Although there is nothing to forgive you for, know that if you feel there is, it is already forgiven, and they/we know that you, with your generous spirit, forgive them/us. The path is clear for you to walk toward the light, gently, with each breath (audibly exhale); you can let your spirit go to follow its path. With each breath, you can let your spirit go to follow its path. With loving arms and open hands we release you. (Pause) With loving arms and open hands we release you. It is okay for you to let go into the open loving arms that are waiting for you (pause). It is okay for you to let go into the open loving arms that are waiting for you. Walk toward the light, Dee. Walk toward the light."

Please bear in mind that this was not read as a script. The healer first put herself in the place of presence and connection before saying the words, and modified the language to resonate both with her client and herself. The tone of voice and the intention are as important as the language itself.

KISS

When God gives life He exhales our first breath into our nostrils[1], and at death He inhales our last breath with a kiss.[2]

---

[1] Genesis 2:7

[2] Deuteronomy 34:5

ELOQUENT GOODBYE

Now a lawyer dealing with egg donations and birth, many years ago she had been a nurse working in hospice. She recounted a story, which thirty years later still made her weep with gratitude:

She was a student nurse being trained in the administration of medications and how to keep up with the mounds of paperwork that went with the task. She recounted how she trailed the head nurse who walked into a hospital room of a man dying from throat cancer, using a chirpy, happy voice and talking to the patient as if he were going to attend a party soon. The student nurse recalls the patient looking at her with sadness, and she reached out her hand to him, which he grasped. Many a night, she would go and sit with him, holding his hand with one of her hands while using the other hand bent over her paperwork at the hospital side table tending to her forms. "I never let go of his hand," she said. "I knew it gave him comfort to feel held, even though I was working on something else. It eased his sense of isolation just to have my presence and my touch." One night, as she was holding his hand, his grip relaxed and he let go. Looking up from her paperwork, she knew that he had passed away, and she squeezed this hand so familiar to her, which was now lifeless. "He never spoke to me with his voice because he was physically unable to," she said. "But he knew I was there for him, and I knew he was grateful for my presence." The lawyer wept.

Letting go was his eloquent goodbye.

LAUGHTER IN THE FACE OF ADVERSITY

They told me not to do the funeral, but I had asked him, and he said he wanted me to do it if I could — who else but me? I tried the night before to write my husband Michael's eulogy but the words wouldn't come. Suddenly, sitting bolt upright in bed at five o'clock in the morning, I wrote and wrote and wrote, and then got dressed carefully for the funeral. I don't remember the drive. I remember getting there and the funeral coach arriving. The funeral director called me over and put her finger to her lips. "Hush, hush, I thought you'd like to see," she said. She lifted the lid of the casket, pulled back the shroud, and I got a glimpse of Michael's head from the crown down. His beard had grown since he had died five days before in the hospital room. Shards of pottery were on his eyes. It is the last image that I have of him and I wish I hadn't seen it.

I called for the start of the funeral. We followed the casket to the grave and I shed no visible tears. I wanted to honor him and be strong for my children, and I was doing what I knew how to do. Hundreds of people and the military were there. The week before Michael died I had changed into my clergy suit in his hospital room to go to officiate at a veteran's funeral. When I saw what the military did, I was so impressed with them that I had gone back to his hospital room afterwards and asked Michael, a Vietnam veteran, that question: "Do you want the 21-gun salute? Do you want me to do the funeral if you die?" How callous does that seem now? But oh, I needed to ask because I needed to know, and I had spent his whole illness barely mentioning the possibility of death just in case it would interfere with the positive healing attitude he was clinging to life with. Looking back, I realize that I did not serve either of us well by not allowing some semblance of reality to prevail. I was doing what I knew how to do. This was part of my goodbye.

And so Michael's funeral began. The military added ceremony and honor to this Jewish funeral, and I was glad they were there, despite my pacifist views. I sang the Hebrew prayers, read the eulogy, and called upon others who wanted to speak. Then, just as we were about to lower the casket into the ground, a man fainted. Suddenly, the flow of the funeral and its tone changed and was not what I had expected to deal with. But how much of my life was ever what I expected to deal with? It seems that just when I am doing what is expected or handling something that is thrown my way, something else comes and I have to handle that, too. So there I was, calling 911 and giving them directions to the cemetery in the middle of my husband's funeral. The man was okay; it was simply too hot and he hadn't eaten breakfast after taking medication. No one was doing crowd control. I had to rescue this funeral! I looked at Michael's casket and I was reminded of our wedding day. I turned back to the microphone, and while the paramedics were taking care of the fallen man, I ushered in the crowd to listen, and said, "If Michael were here among us now, he'd be taking care of this situation. In fact, I am sure Michael would find the irony and humor that even his funeral is not the norm. You see, on our wedding day, as we entered the parking lot of the synagogue, the building next door was on fire and we had to wait for the firemen to put out the fire before we got married." The crowd chuckled. They paid attention, and I was able to finish conducting the funeral.

Our wedding, his funeral, both with the highly unexpected coming up, both handled with humor. What about that other lifecycle event—birth? After our second child was born, the hospital wanted me to put the baby in a car seat for the ride home, but I wanted to carry him in my arms. The nurses insisted and I acquiesced. Not fifteen minutes from the hospital on Pacific Coast Highway, we were faced with a car going the wrong direction coming full-speed toward us, and before we had time to scream, we were in a head-on collision. Reclining in the passenger seat, I slipped down under the seat belt onto the floor and into the dashboard. I heard Michael shouting that he couldn't see because his glasses had been knocked off, and he couldn't move his arm. Our five-year-old in the back seat was holding his forehead and crying and the newborn baby was fast asleep. The car seat had not budged. The children were fine. We were transported back to the hospital where I had just given birth, and despite our injuries, I joked with my obstetrician that he hadn't put enough stitches in my rear end so I came back for more. Michael joked with the nurses about giving the car seat a crash test. We both had injuries that never completely healed, and many lessons to learn about the courage of dealing with adversity along the way.

When the unexpected happens, laughter is sometimes the best way to summon courage. I hope it will strengthen my children when I am gone.

MIDWIFE

It was a cold Seattle morning. We sat in the First Covenant Church, cradling our cups of tea in our hands and waiting for the speaker we came to listen to ascend the podium to speak. We had fortuitously secured a front row pew, getting as close as possible to see and hear the pearls of wisdom that we knew were going to come from David Whyte. We were not disappointed.

When I listen to Mr. Whyte's recordings, which is daily, I often have to stop the recording because much of what he says I want to stop and think about and turn over in my mind, and he is so profound that I don't want to miss a word of what comes next. I had flown especially from California to Seattle to attend his full-day seminar, which was entitled, "Solace: The Art of Asking The Beautiful Question." At first, I attempted to take notes, but just like with the recordings, I didn't want to miss a word, and now that I was listening to him in person, I decided simply to enjoy each word as it came, trusting that I would remember what I needed to remember, and only making the odd note here and there. Several times during the day, Mr. Whyte paused, gave us a question to ponder, and asked us to discuss it with our neighbor. My neighbor to my left was my son William, who had joined me on this "bucket list" trip, and to my right was Laura, a midwife who lived locally. My son and I decided to speak with strangers so that they would no longer be strangers and we could then expand our perspectives. During one of our discussions, Laura described to me a phenomenon she had seen in many of the births she had attended.

She said that when a mother is in the transition phase of labor, there comes a pivotal moment when she realizes that no matter who is there, it is only the mother and her body that can give birth to the child. Laura said it is as if a light bulb is turned on and the mother instinctively knows that there is no turning back, and that she is totally alone in the process; she must both push and let go of the child who is to be born. Laura said she could see that struggle on the face of her mothers. It reminded me of some of the deaths at which I had been present, where I can see it in the breathing pattern. When someone is dying there, too, comes a transition point at which no matter who is there with the person, the soul struggles to leave the body, while the body both struggles to hold on and let go. I see birth and death as opposite ends of the same spectrum. Who knows if this life we live is a gestation for another world beyond this life? As Mr. Whyte so eloquently put it to us that day, "Death is one dynamic we are not supposed to understand, but we have to live in its presence."

PRESENCE IN SILENCE

I was in the middle of eating dinner on my day off when I was called by a hospice company to go to the bedside of a 26-year-old woman dying of breast cancer. I put down my fork, gathered up my keys and my prayer book and went to the woman's house. When I arrived and observed the situation, I realized that it was not my voice or my prayers that were needed. It was my touch and my presence for a person wrestling in the last few hours of life, and my focused attention as her father poured out his anguish. As she reached out her arms to me and clutched my hands, I said nothing. I held her hands, stroked her head devoid of hair, and focused on her eyes. Being silent yet mindfully present is a form of prayer.

LIFE IS A HOLY TEXT

Many are familiar with The Lord's Prayer, which begins "Our Father, which art in heaven, hallowed be thy name." This prayer originated from the Aramaic prayer known in Judaism as the Kaddish. Kaddish means "Holiness." The prayer originated as something one said after studying a holy text. There are five different versions of the Kaddish, and whenever it is placed in a service, it signifies that something has come to an end and something else is beginning.

One of the Kaddish prayers, known as the Mourner's Kaddish, is said after someone dies. Saying Kaddish after someone has died is honoring life in the same way we honor any holy text. The Kaddish prayer, written in Aramaic, does not mention death; rather, the prayer praises the Author of life. This is what you have been doing in your long goodbye, praising the life of the one who is before you and may be no more. There will be time for Kaddish later. For now, it is time to say goodbye, like the ending of a long beloved book that you do not want to put down and do not want to end: When you close the final chapter and marvel at the conclusion of this particular journey, you can anticipate that having read and experienced the book, it will never ever leave you long after it has been read.

IN SPIRIT'S SERVICE

Everywhere I have turned this week, both in my professional and personal life, people have been experiencing loss. Likewise, others have been experiencing uplifting joy. As they reach out to me or I to them, the intense focus and need to balance informs me. One thing I have received with great clarity: Spirit always places me exactly where I need to be in its service.

SELF-CARE

IS SELF-CARE SELFISH?

If you have ever flown on an airplane, you will know that at the beginning of each and every flight you will be instructed that in the event of loss of air pressure in the cabin to "put your own oxygen mask on first before offering assistance to another." This same principle applies to caring for yourself in everyday life, and is particularly crucial when in crisis—both when caring for someone who is ill, as well as after loss. You cannot help someone else if you are not able to breathe. Self-care and nurturing your emotional and physical well-being is not selfish. It is, in fact, the only way to be truly altruistic and loving, because you will be able to give more when you are coming from a position of strength. You will also set an example for others, so that they in turn can help you.

Caring for yourself when you are caring for those who are ill or dependent on you is different than caring for yourself after loss, although many of the tactics you employ will be the same. When someone is depending on you to care for them, you may forget to put yourself first because their need seems to be more critical than yours. When you have suffered a loss and no one is depending on you, you may not feel like caring for yourself, particularly in the early stages of grief, and it won't seem to make much difference if you don't. When you have suffered a loss and you still have others depending on you, grief can make it more difficult to care for them.

Self-care means to take care of all of your self. You need to pay attention to get enough sleep, eat healthfully, exercise, and play. Anticipating your needs ahead of time can be tremendously helpful in caring for yourself. When Michael was first diagnosed, my adrenalin kicked into high gear, and I was so intent on taking care of him that I forgot I was hungry until my stomach hurt, and realized that I was not getting enough sleep only when I started to doze off while driving. So I anticipated my needs by routinely carrying protein bars, fruit, and nuts in my bag so I could eat in a doctor's waiting room. When I made meals, I doubled up on them so that I did not have to prepare the next day, and I always had healthy food available in the refrigerator because Michael did not have an appetite while undergoing chemotherapy, and in the moments when he did, there was no time to prepare the food—it needed to be ready, or his appetite would be gone by the time the food was prepared, and stopping at a fast food place was not a healthy option. It took thinking ahead and anticipating what would be needed so that when it was needed, it was there.

I learned to go for my run when I had settled Michael in his chair for several hours of chemotherapy, and I always had a bag packed with snacks and activities for him as well as for myself. I would make lists. Lots of lists. Sometimes I would put something mundane on the list like "get dressed" just so I could cross it off and feel a sense of accomplishment. And there were days when getting dressed was quite an accomplishment!

I learned to write notes to myself. Not the to-do list kind of notes, but the loving positive notes that said things like, "You are doing well today, Sue. Breathe." Or "You are not alone, look up!" Five years after Michael's death, I still write notes to myself. Whenever I leave the house to travel, I always write myself a welcome home note, knowing that I will be walking into an empty house and that this little note will remind me that I am cared for. I now look forward to those notes because I can never remember what I wrote!

After loss, caring for oneself can be difficult during the process of grief. It really helps to have a network of people who can offer support, either by bringing a meal, grocery shopping, giving you a listening ear, or helping you with practical matters like cleaning, organizing, and paperwork. Learning to ask for help and receive it from others was extremely difficult for me to do. In fact, this section of this book was written last because I had so much difficulty in understanding self-care, how to ask for help, and how to receive help.

There were tasks I had to do that were time-consuming and I knew that I needed expert help, and so I hired people to help me. Just as I hire a mechanic to change the oil in my car because I don't know how to do it myself, I hire people to do the things I cannot do. I hired a professional organizer to help me go through 30 years of living in my house and organize the mountain of possessions that Michael and my children did not throw away. I consult with a life coach to help me understand what my life path is and how to live my best life.

There was no life insurance when Michael died. I still had a dependent child. I am not wealthy. I put enlisting the help of others as one of the priorities in my expenses right up there with food. Sometimes it feels like I spend most of my income on hiring others, but in the end, it is part of self-care and moving forward. None of us exist in a vacuum, even though we may feel like it.

I came to understand that by asking someone for help, I was giving them the opportunity to do something for me and feel good about it. I also came to understand that if someone turns me down, it may be because what I am asking of them is not possible for them to do at that time, and I need not take it personally. At such times, I either need to ask someone else, or hire someone to help me.

I learned to say "thank you" when given a gift without feeling like I had to rush out and buy a gift in return, knowing that if it was meant to be, the time would come when I would have the opportunity to reciprocate or pay that gift forward to someone else, or simply appreciate it because it was meant for me.

Most of all, working in a service profession and being a caregiver by nature, I had to learn to say "no" when what I was being asked to do would negatively affect my well-being. Just as when I accept help I know I am giving someone an opportunity to do something for me, I know that by saying "no" to someone else, I am saying "yes" to myself. It took reaching the point of exhaustion to be able to say "no", and to recognize that taking care of myself was not being selfish. Moreover, the more I say yes to myself, the more I am able to give, in the long run, to someone else.

GETTING OUT OF BED WHEN IT IS
DIFFICULT TO DO SO

There may be days when you will wake up and not want to get out of bed, not because you are ill or you didn't get enough sleep, but simply because you do not want to face the day, and when you think of the future, it seems an impossible load to bear. At these times, it helps to do something that gives you comfort by keeping you in the present moment. Tell yourself that you don't have to get up just yet. Just be with yourself for a moment. Cuddle a pillow or something soft, turn over, and as you hold the soft object, imagine for a moment that it is holding you. Then think of it as a baby carrier on your chest and pack it with your hurting self. Tell it that you will keep it safe throughout the day and you will not abandon it.

Think now only of this one minute. In this minute, place one foot outside the bed, but do not put it on the floor yet. Slowly peel back the sheets and blankets from the bed, and now thinking only about this moment, not the whole day ahead, put your other foot on the edge of the bed, and together place them on the floor as you come to a sitting position. Now slowly rise to stand on your two feet. Look down at your feet. Tell your feet that they are now going to walk to the bathroom, and as you walk, feel the self that you are cherishing in that carrier on your chest. It is safe with you. You carry yourself and your own protection whenever you need it, from moment to moment.

Once you have made the initial step out of bed, each successive moment will become a little easier if you think only of minute to minute. When comfortable with that, you can increase the time span, if you wish. Whenever future thinking makes you feel like you want to dive back under the covers and you don't have that luxury, bring yourself back to the present moment. Look at that future thinking as a wave, one that will pass, and that what you have to do is allow the wave to wash over you and float with the current. Knowing that the wave will pass, trusting that even if you cannot swim, you can always float, and even if the current pulls you under, it is only for a moment, because you will rise to the top simply by letting go of the future and focusing on and feeling the present moment. It is the most precious moment, and you are its jewel.

SPIRITUAL MUSCLE

As I pumped iron at the gym this morning, it occurred to me that if I held onto the weight instead of pushing through the resistance, it would take far more energy and leave my muscles fatigued without growth. Sometimes that resistance seems so insurmountable and pushing could cause injury, in which case, yielding and letting go is the best course of action. Listening to the body is key. So it is with spiritual muscle.

THE BEACH

There are days at work when I stare death in the face and yet again become intimate with its call. At the close of these days, I sometimes choose to come down to the beach at dusk and pour some sacred teardrops into God's vast ocean. As I watch the seagulls fly and the people play, I remind myself that the sand I am sitting and standing on is made up of particles that shift with the ebb and flow of the tide, and that it is not I who made the beach.

Sue Knight Deutsch

WORDS AND THE LANGUAGE OF DEATH

Words are so important. When Rabbi Bradley Shavit Artson taught me how to conduct a funeral, he instructed me to be careful with the words I used. "It is earth, not dirt; a casket, not a coffin; a coach, not a hearse," he said. Years later, when I trained to learn how to ritually prepare a body for burial, David Zinner also instructed that words and language are important, specifying the denotation and connotation of words. "We 'lovingly bathe the deceased' rather than 'wash the body'; we 'carefully dress' rather than 'assemble the shrouds'; 'spiritual' is more comfortable than 'ritual'; 'loving, sensitive and caring' rather than 'traditional,'" he said. As I entered the room where the loving bathing takes place, surveyed the ceramic platform and all the equipment, including the casket, I noticed a sign on the wall. In red it said, "Remember!" and underneath there was a caution to be mindful of the fact that you are in the presence of someone precious, someone who is the child, parent, spouse or sibling of someone else. Be respectful and loving and treat that person as if the family were in attendance with you, it read.

As I surveyed that preparation room and I thought back on all the language I had been advised to use around the death process, it occurred to me — wouldn't the world be a gentler place if we spoke to people in life the way we take precaution to speak in death? Once again death teaches us about life. Words and language are indeed important.

THE TALE OF THE THREE-LEGGED DOG

For the last twenty-eight years I have either walked or jogged around my neighborhood virtually every morning, at times with a child or two in a stroller, come rain or shine. It is interesting that despite journeying on the same route every day, there are so many different things to notice, either about the houses or the streets or the people in the houses and on the streets. Through the years I have come to know my neighbors and have become familiar with their lives and their families. I know which dogs are friendly and which ones to avoid. I pass by the park at the top of the main street of the neighborhood and know that if I go out early in the winter while it is still dark, I may see a coyote or two hanging out there. I almost always take the same route, unless I am avoiding an animal that I sense may attack. I have only been bitten once, and that was by a dog that was on a leash. For years, I used to see a dog in the park that walked with a strange gait being walked by his owner. I never looked too closely, but I did notice that the dog had its front left leg missing. I never thought much about it, other than that I saw it once in a while.

When Michael became sick, I continued my daily run through the neighborhood, and on the days when he had chemotherapy for several hours, I would run for an hour around the neighborhood near the oncology clinic. Continuing to run helped me to cope with my life which felt like it was unraveling, and gave me a space to let my thoughts run free and my tears fall. After Michael died, I went back to running in my neighborhood exclusively. In the early stages of my grief process, I felt like an amputee. Having been married to Michael for over thirty-one years, being without him felt like I was missing a limb. I would wonder while running how on earth I would ever learn to live alone and if I would ever feel whole again.

One morning as I was running by the park, I saw the three-legged dog again. This time, I stopped and watched as the dog ran on his three legs, chasing a ball his owner had thrown. I walked up to the owner and asked him about the dog. The dog's name was Cody, and his owner, Roger, had found him by the roadside when he was a puppy, tied up, malnourished and badly injured. Roger had rescued him and took him to a vet, but his leg could not be saved. Cody was taught how to walk on three legs. I was so inspired by the sight of this loving and gentle animal walking on three legs, and I knew that if Cody could do it, so could I.

Roger knew that Cody was an inspiration. He felt that in rescuing Cody, there was an opportunity not only to help the injured dog, but for Cody and his story to serve others in a meaningful way. Cody was trained as a therapy dog, and Roger takes him to hospitals and nursing homes where he is showered with love and inspires those who need to see that even with a missing limb, walking forward into life is possible. At my invitation, Roger and Cody are now regular visitors at the assisted living facility where I work. I continue to journey through my neighborhood, no longer feeling like an amputee, and looking closely at everything and everyone I see, stopping to ask them questions and connect to life.

ASK FOR AN ADVOCATE:
Caregiver becomes the patient

When I visit someone in the hospital I try to imagine how it might feel to be a patient. I am always glad to see visitors in the room and delighted to know that the patient has an advocate. I am fortunate to be quite healthy. It has been a long time since I have had to have medical attention other than to go to the doctor for regular checkups. Some of the checkup procedures make me feel vulnerable, and when weakened by illness and pain, this vulnerability can be magnified. I used to run five miles daily until one day I twisted my leg and injured my knee. Living alone and too proud to ask anyone to come to the doctor with me, I went alone. Just the experience of being alone while injured was enough to make me feel vulnerable and frustrated. I thought of the people I minister to who do not have anyone they can call. The following experience taught me to reach out and ask for help and brought home that no person's pain can be measured by another's, and that when we need help, we must ask for it and be able to receive it.

In the waiting room:

Sitting here in the orthopedist's waiting room. It is a nicely furnished office, beautifully situated, in upscale Newport Beach. Clinically cold. I am surrounded by people in massive pain. I feel it coming at me from every angle. The man with the newly broken arm who is trying so hard to be brave; the girl with her leg in a splint from ankle to pelvis who thinks her mother is annoying; the man with the sad face who feels helpless and vulnerable in his wheelchair; the woman leaning on a walker with a bandage on her knee who wishes her arms were stronger. Each patient has someone with them to help, to talk to them, to ease their pain, simply to be with them.

Each and every one of them has someone—not one of them is here on their own as I am. What am I doing here? I am not suffering like they are. I am not in as much as pain as they are. I am sitting here in a nice business suit with my laptop on my knees, my leg muscles on fire, and my little hurt knee says, "You came here so you could take care of me. You have to take care of me so I can take care of you. You are all there is. Want someone to hold your hand, Sue? That is what teaches you to extend your hand to another. You are the reason you stand alone."

Oh I want to run far away from here, and then my knee reminds me: I am in pain, I cannot run, and although I have no one to accompany me, it does not make me less deserving than anyone else, and the fact that I am not suffering the way they are doesn't make me special either. Yet still, I want the earth to open and swallow me up, and I know that I am the reason I feel this way.

I walk down the long hallway, following a uniformed aide to the exam room. He is walking so quickly that it is painful for me to keep up with him, but I don't say so and I don't show it. Other aides pass by in the hallway; they are all wearing navy polo shirts and khaki trousers. They are young and fit; they use hair gel; they move quickly in business-like fashion, and they remind me of bellhops.

In the exam room, after interview by doctor's aide, before x-rays:

The aide asked me how I am. I told him I am fine. Oh wait, my knee hurts! In fact, my whole leg hurts, my hip hurts, and I can't walk properly and I can't run or dance, and I feel like that would be complaining, so I say, "Oh, I injured my knee, and I'm here for a diagnosis so I can know how to take care of myself." So he tells me that insurance will require x-rays before they can do an MRI, and it will take 5 days for authorization for an MRI.

What? I pay for $400 a month for premium PPO insurance! How could this be? He shakes his head and says that PPO insurance actually denies more procedures than HMOs. My pain is secondary to the medical business.

In the x-ray room:

The navy-shirted, khaki-trousered young technician with perfect hair tells me how to stand, hands me a lead apron and takes pictures. He doesn't smile. I crack a joke, he doesn't laugh. I wince when he moves my leg. He doesn't react. I feel like a piece of meat. I want to cry.

In the exam room, waiting for the doctor after x-rays:

I am sad and I am afraid and I am alone and I want to be held and even though I feel my angels and Spirit around me, I want a human hand, a human arm. Not the cold, clinical doctor and doctor's aides. I want someone to heal me, not to fix me. I want someone like me to come into this room and hold my hand and tell me all will be well; to connect with me, to look into my eyes and breathe with me, and maybe even sing with me. I want to feel like I matter. And I am not seriously ill or dying! How much more so does someone who is seriously ill or dying need someone like me?

I am the reason I am in pain.

After being examined by the doctor:

The doctor told me that my ACL is fine. That is good. He shrugged his shoulders when I asked if I should be moving or resting, and said he couldn't tell me how to proceed until after he'd seen the MRI, because he doesn't know what is wrong, only what is not wrong. He is in the room with me, but he is not present. This man is not a healer.

I drive home, and on the way I call my massage therapist to share what happened. He advises me to keep moving and listen to my body's cues as I always do. I decide in that call that I need to revamp my insurance and stop paying a fortune for medical treatment. I remember being Michael's advocate. I advocate for others all the time. One more lesson in empathy for those I serve; I step into my power.

I arrive home alone, and in a sea whose waves are pain, I cry.

Are you a caregiver? Who advocates for you? Ask yourself who you might be able to call when you need help. The list you come up with is part of your self-care. Don't forget to put yourself first on the list!

HEALING VISION

As I began to drive 40 miles to officiate at a funeral on a Tuesday, I felt the contact lens in my right eye bothering me. I didn't have time to fiddle with it, so I put some eye drops in to moisten my eye, then jumped in the car, and set up my iPhone so that I could call in to a previously scheduled conference call that I would "attend" during my drive. I returned home that afternoon and my eyes were still bothering me, so I attempted to take my contact lenses out, but I couldn't find the one in my right eye. It certainly felt like it was there, but try as I might, I couldn't locate it, and my eye was becoming really irritated.

I called my optometrist and she told me to come in so she could examine my eye. After searching around with a flashlight, she told me that she couldn't find anything and that because my vision was blurry in that eye, the lens must have fallen out earlier in the day. The next day, I noticed a discharge coming out of that eye, so, still feeling that the contact lens was there, I went to an ophthalmologist to see if he could find it. He also said there was nothing there, that I must have an infection, and gave me antibiotic drops. By Friday, my eye still felt like something was in it, and the drops weren't helping. I had a conversation with someone who upset me, and when I was alone I started to cry. As tears streamed down my face, I felt a release in my eye, and something floating on my eyelid. I reached up, and there it was—my contact lens that two experts had said was not there!

Lessons learned:
- Slow down and listen to my body's signals.
- Trust my intuition over the expert's opinion.

- What I see is not always my best vision, and the truth may be hidden.
- Sometimes the best form of healing is a really good cry.

THE CLIFF'S EDGE

The mountain road winds and turns and I turn the wheels of the car to follow the road. The full moon beckons in the distance as the only light source backlighting the mountain. Black, black on deep blue. I want to stop this journey. Stop driving so that I can breathe in the majestic mountain and feel Spirit in the air around me, to connect with that which is my Creator, the One who propels me on this journey.

I pull over to the side of the road and park at the cliff's edge. Getting out of the car, I stand at the cliff's edge and stare down into the ravine. I listen to the silence broken only by a passing car, a fellow traveler on this journey. I breathe the cool air around me, my ears throbbing with the beat of my heart. I am part of this. This is what I am deep in conversation with, the natural order, part of the pulse that moves from moment to moment. Alone but not alone, as I feel myself cradled by the darkness with a thousand loving eyes seeing me and loving what they see. Many hands and arms and the presence of beings that say, "Welcome, welcome to this Universe. So glad you paused on the journey to take note of that which is always here to love and support you."

As I feel my feet move slowly back to my car, I pick up my journey. The moon winks at me and the mountain stands firm, and all Creation whispers: "Come back home whenever you need to. We are always here holding space for you, Beloved."

I ATE AN EGG

I ate an egg this morning. It was soft boiled, and I took some fresh baked bread, which I made into toast soldiers and dipped them into the gooey yolk. The egg just looked so good that I could not resist it. I needed to be kind to myself to allow myself to eat it, yet I am vegan. But the egg held a memory. A childhood memory of the comfort and safety of my mother's kitchen, being loved and cared for, and its taste brought back the long-lost sensation of being held. An egg! An egg that could have become a bird had its mother warmed and hatched it. Had it become a bird, it would have grown wings and learned to fly. But I ate the egg, and that was part of my initiation into growing wings, vegan though I may be.

A SEAPLANE, KAYAK, AND
DEEP SEA DARKNESS

People told me that flying in a seaplane could be scary. One person said that sitting in the back would make it less scary because I wouldn't be able to see much. One person said that sitting up front would be the best because I could see everything. I had never flown in a seaplane before, and here I was, going on an adventure, flying to Hollyhock on Cortes Island in a little seaplane that seated six. I was excited at the prospect. Never being one to hide, I decided I would like to see everything and sit up front. Before we climbed into the little plane, I asked the pilot if I could sit up front with him, and he agreed. I was elated. Even before takeoff, I was exhilarated just to sit in the seat right next to the pilot with all the little dials and controls in front of me and a clear full panoramic view of the ocean.

The seaplane skimmed the ocean before it took off, and the noise was so loud that earplugs only muffled the sound a little. We communicated by gesturing in an improvised sign language, and before long, the plane was in the air. I marveled at how we were high enough that things on the ground looked small, but not high enough that they disappeared. I imagined how it must feel to be a bird, and how insignificant all the little details of being human on the ground were at that very moment.

Despite a lifelong fear of deep water, the seaplane ride was thrilling for me. I felt safe in the hands of the pilot and overjoyed to have this perspective of the earth I feel so connected to. Day-to-day concerns seemed so trivial from this vantage point.

Once at Hollyhock, I was offered an opportunity to go bioluminescent kayaking. In this adventure, a small group of people paddled kayaks out into the sea late at night to see the bioluminescent sea life that sparkled in the water. I signed up. I was one of four people in our kayaking party, including our guide. I am not sure why, but until I got to the edge of the water and our guide was demonstrating how to put on our lifejackets and water-proof skirts, and then how to roll with the kayak should we capsize, it had not occurred to me that I would be kayaking in deep water. Deep ocean water. Suddenly, I became afraid. What if I capsized and couldn't swim? What if I drowned? What if? What if? As always, when I feel fear, I ask it what it wants to teach me. Sometimes, the fear is there to protect me, and sometimes it is so great that I allow it the power to change what I am doing, not always in my best interests.

As I stood on the seashore looking at the kayak and the instructor, I decided there was no turning back. I was not going to sit this one out. I thanked my fear for trying to protect me, and told it that I was going to trust that I would be all right. Hadn't the Universe shown me so, over and over? With my heart pounding, I lowered myself into the kayak, snapped my skirt into place, moved the paddle according to the guide's instructions, and we set off. Before long, we were in the middle of the ocean watching the most glorious sunset. The only sound I could hear was the sound of my paddle in the water, my breathing, and the occasional comment as the four of us marveled at the experience.

Before long, darkness fell. With no city lights, it was so dark that we could barely see in front of us. We put fluorescent tubes around our heads so that we could locate each other in the black night. With each stroke of the paddle, the ocean came to life. I was fascinated by what appeared to be underwater fireworks, and even more fascinated that if I had not made any movement in the water, I would never have seen those sea creatures. It made me think of the times in both real and spiritual dark-ness when it either appears that nothing is there, or that something malevolent is out to get me. As a child, fearful of the dark, one of my foster parents had told me that nothing is there in the darkness that is not in the light. There, sitting in a kayak in the darkness, floating on the deep ocean, I knew that everything was there in the darkness that I could not see in the light.

At one point, my party of kayakers paddled way ahead of me and I was left alone in the darkness. Because of the time of year and the absence of city lights, I could see the Milky Way, and the stars were huge and brilliant and I felt like I could pluck them from the sky. I leaned back in my kayak and looked up at the night sky. The silence and stillness was palpable. It was so quiet that I could hear my pulse in my head as my blood was pumped through my body, and suddenly, I clearly felt that I was as much a part of Creation as were the stars. The sense of Oneness and Connection felt like I was not restricted by the boundaries of my body. I was fully a part of Creation.

There are times in my life now when tasks seem to constrict me, and everyday stress and darkness descends upon me, and then I take myself back to that time in the seaplane with a bird's eye view of the earth, and to the kayak, floating in the darkness on the deep blue ocean. I forgive myself for all the times I allowed fear to get in the way of the deep knowing that I am part of Creation, I will always be all right, and that the mystery of the darkness will bring me peace and light my way.

BE AT EASE

My roommate hugged me goodbye. We had known each other a mere 48 hours and yet she said that being in my presence was something that would stay with her. We had lots of laughs and heart-to-heart talks, but most of all, she thanked me for my calming effect in the middle of the night. I had forgotten that she had woken me in the night with her shouting, and I did not remember what I had said or done, so she reminded me. She had awoken shouting, thinking that she had heard a crash. Her shouting woke me up, and when I said I had not heard anything but her, she recognized that it had been a dream. In the darkness, she was moaning and breathing heavily, and apparently I spoke to her in a calming voice, telling her to slow her breathing and saying softly, "Be at ease, be at ease." I recognize those words as the ones spoken to me by one of my healing teachers, Bev Martin, and I marveled that I had so well absorbed them that they came out of my mouth in the midst and haze of my slumber.

Was that really me speaking, or Spirit speaking through me? And when my teacher speaks to me, is it Spirit speaking through her? We are all connected through this invisible thread. How comforting to know that it is for the greater good, and that even in the darkness it holds space for us.

WHISPER TO A SHOUT

My legs hurt. I had just returned from vacation and the ache I felt in my legs while I was running every morning had turned into major pain. My muscles finally gave way and tore when I ignored the warning signals. The last time I was in that much physical pain was when I broke my toe right before High Holy Days in 2007. I blamed Michael for leaving a box just enough out of the line of sight outside our bathroom for me to walk into, and so I moved out of the bedroom while I was healing. He spent many a day beating his chest in repentance, especially when he watched me standing for hours in a surgical boot on the pulpit. I broke a toe the year after he died, and with only myself to blame, I thought I had learned my lesson then. But no, now with torn knees and hamstrings as Passover approached, Spirit came to remind me just when I needed it most, that when you don't listen to the whisper, the lesson will be presented in another way, and it will shout, "Pay attention!"

THE PROCESS OF GRIEF: ANOTHER HEALING HAND

WHEN WILL YOU GET OVER IT?

Less than a month after my husband died, some-one at work asked me, "So, are you over it yet?" Stunned, I didn't know how to answer. Everyone grieves differ-ently. I could talk to you about grief; about hurting so much that it is painful to be in your own skin; about going from what feels like screaming agony to a dull ache. I could write a whole book about grief. However, there are a plethora of books written on the stages of grief, on how to manage grief, on what grief feels like, so for now, I in-clude just a few stories that have come to me in my grieving process. Although everyone grieves differently, grief is universal in that we will all experience it at one time or another, as no one lives without loss at some point.

One thing I have learned for sure—grief is a pro-cess, and the only way out is through. As painful as grief is, it is a healing process. If you have had the opportunity to address the conversations in the earlier part of this book, some of your process will have begun and may pro-vide some solace. If you did not have the opportunity, all is not lost! You can have these same conversations even if your loved one is no longer here. The difference is that you will have to imagine the responses of your loved one, but it is the process and content of the conversation that is important. Imagine how often you project what you think onto someone else, only to discover that they are not thinking what you are projecting. The process is the same with someone who has died, only your projections can now provide the answers that you need to hear. Voic-ing something aloud gives it an energy and power.

The 5 discussions to have with the dying who are living do something besides ease the process; they help to ease any regret that may occur after a loved one has died. I had regret after my husband died even when I had addressed all the issues in these discussions.

One regret I had was that Michael never got to go to China. One of Michael's passions was martial arts, and he earned a teaching credential in Tai Chi. He had always wanted to go to practice and study with some of the Tai Chi masters in China, and an opportunity came up two years before he died. Although our finances were limited, it was on his "bucket list," and so we attended the meeting where the trip was being planned. We were arranging where our daughter would stay, and how much everything would cost, and then we discovered that the dates coincided with a Jewish holy day where I would be required to be on my pulpit, and it would further deplete our finances if I took the time off. Michael said, "Never mind, Sue. There'll be another trip in two years. Alexandra will be in college then, and we'll be in a better position to take the trip." The trip did indeed come up again, but Michael was gone.

When Michael was diagnosed, he asked the oncologist if he could make the trip to China and arrange to have chemotherapy there, and was told that he could only travel if he went into remission. I asked Michael to forgive me for putting everything else before his one wish to take that trip. He told me that it was his choice to put it off, and he did not feel it was my fault, so there was nothing to forgive me for. He said he had no regret about making the decision, only that he did not have the foresight to go to China sooner. Yet still, every time I took a trip somewhere after he died, I would feel immense guilt and regret over China.

It came to a head on my 56th birthday, which was the age Michael never lived to see. I even felt regret over living longer than him! I specifically went to Esalen for that birthday so that I could be in a place that supported me. My back started hurting when I went to bed on the night of my birthday. I looked out of the window of my room where there was a waterfall, and the moon was shining, the sky brightly lit with stars, and I felt Michael's presence. I started to cry and told him how terrible I felt for spending the money he had worked so hard to save and had not spent on himself. How awful it was that I was living longer than he was and enjoying my life! I heard him answer me in my head. "Sue, that is what I earned the money for. You are walking forward into life and carrying me with you, even though no one can see me. This is exactly what I want you to do! Spend the money doing what you love! Don't wait for your China!"

When will you get over it? You won't. You will walk through it. Forward, step by step, into life. With each wave of grief, you will either float, swim, or struggle. Waves pass, and there will be calmer waters, even as there may be more waves ahead.

What follows are stories I wrote during the first five years of my grief journey, and just so you know, I am still walking forward with Michael. There is a smile on my face, and although you can't see it, I can see that there is a smile on his face, too.

WHAT IS THE PURPOSE OF FEAR?

Though I felt quite fearful as I left the parking garage and the GPS hadn't yet recognized that it was in Oregon, I decided to just drive forward and see where I ended up. Then the directions came up. I was a little suspicious because the GPS wouldn't accept the actual address, but as the fear came up, I breathed into it and surrendered to the Unknown. That wonderful calm came over me and I just followed the directions, taking the time to drink in my surroundings and notice the landscape. Before long, I recognized where I was, and lo and behold, there was a parking spot big enough for me to parallel park on the street. Such a sense of peace and elation came over me because my trusting had once again shown me that I am held, and I am held beautifully. The question is, what purpose does the fear serve?

THE BRIDGE OF THE GODS:
Discerning the purpose of fear

The name of the bridge piqued my interest. I had heard about it from a friend who read about it in a novel by Cheryl Strayed, and knowing that I go to Oregon often, suggested that I go there on a hike.

On one of my longer stays in Portland, I rented a car and invited a friend to go hiking with me on the Pacific Crest Trail right by the Bridge Of The Gods. But first, I wanted to walk across the bridge, which is the way to cross over the Columbia River from Oregon to Washington. We drove from Portland on a beautiful summer's day and parked down below the bridge, then walked up to the booth at the beginning of the bridge. It was 50 cents to walk across, and $1 to go by car. We paid our 50 cents and approached the bridge. The tollbooth operator advised us to keep close to the side of the bridge, as there was no walking lane, and to walk against oncoming traffic. As we approached the beginning of the bridge, we were pushed back by strong winds, so strong that we had to lean in to the wind in order to move forward. Once on the bridge, the floor beneath our feet was a metal grid through which we could see straight through to the river below us. Although beautiful, there was a sense of being suspended in mid-air rather than grounded. Coupled with the strong wind that made me hold fast to the side railings of the bridge, I became afraid. My friend had already turned back. I looked across the bridge, trying to see how far I would have to walk, wondering what would happen if I felt unsafe when I was right in the middle of the bridge, and asked myself this question: "Is this fear something I should push through, or is it warning me that I am not safe?" As the traffic drove so close by me that I could almost reach out and touch the cars, I decided to turn back and err on the side of safety.

Once back off the bridge, I realized with dismay that I had not taken a photograph. I wanted a photograph! So I walked back to the tollbooth and asked if I might go back just to take a photograph. Again, I approached the bridge, and again, the winds drove my body backward. As I stood with one hand holding the railing and the other trying to hold and focus the camera in the wind, I pointed the camera lens down at my feet to try to capture that sense of suspension. Again I felt the fear, only this time it was stronger. It assured me that the purpose of this fear was to keep me safe. I still wanted to cross over the bridge. I walked back to the car where my friend was waiting and I drove across the bridge while she took pictures. Another lesson learned: when fear signals me that the journey feels unsafe, I can get to where I want to go by choosing a safer mode of transport.

DESPITE TRANSFORMATION

Despite transformation, moving forward, standing and thriving in the full height of who I am, when October rolls around with its memories of my beloved's sudden illness, the long gnarled tentacles of grief curl themselves around my heart and hold it in their grip. Then shards of darkness creep up and cast a shadow on my soul. My heart, still beating, whispers: "Where there is shadow, you will find light."

WHERE THE GRASS IS GREEN

I am not a jealous person, although I admit that when I walk around my neighborhood in the morning I look wistfully at the runners who pass by me and I am filled with longing. I long to have my healthy legs back and run again. Then I turn the corner and see Jeb, the blind old man who walks with his walker every morning, stopping to rest and to listen to his world. I stop to talk to him every day, and did so even when I was running. I am part of his world and he is part of mine. He reminds me of Michael, 30 years his junior, who used to sit and rest with his walker and talk to Jeb about his cancer and how he longed to be strong and healthy again, and about his struggle just to make it around the block. Jeb remembers Michael, even though Michael died a few years ago. Longing and struggle are both part of the same package; one is the impetus for the other. I pat my legs in appreciation that they allow me to walk unaided. We are gifted with each other to see, even if blind, how it could be and how it might be in either direction.

THROUGH WHICH LENS?

It was a room with a balcony overlooking the ocean. Meant to be a shared room, I was thrilled to find myself arriving on personal retreat with no roommate assigned to my room and me therefore free to dump my stuff where I wished, keep the hours I wanted with no mind for anyone else's personal space, and to pick the best bed right by the window with the glorious view. Imagine my surprise when 24 hours later I came back to the room to find someone in the other bed. She was a lovely lady, and we had much in common both in habits and preferences, and I thanked the Universe for sending me such a compatible roommate. As she nestled down to sleep, I went to the hot tubs to watch the stars in their nightly heavenly parade, and to whisper in the darkness to the Creator of such majesty, quietly discussing the constellations and our journeys to the stars with my fellow bathers.

I came back to the room with a little flashlight guiding my way in the darkness, very tired and relaxed, and got ready for bed, removing my contact lenses, cleaning them and putting them back in their blue-and-white case. When I opened the case, there were contacts already in it. Puzzled, I chided myself for bringing an old pair with me, and placed the case in the zippered compartment of my wash bag so that the two pairs would not get mixed up, and placed the current contacts in the empty case. Morning came, and I sat up in bed watching the sunrise over the ocean, lost in my thoughts. My roommate awoke to her alarm and got ready to go to yoga. I told her I was going to spend the morning with my writing and would see her at breakfast. She came out of the bathroom blinking and said that there was something wrong with her contacts, or maybe her eyes were dry, but she couldn't see properly and she had to put a new pair in. Deeply buried in my thoughts, I didn't make the connection that there had been a mix-up until I went to put my contacts in and realized that the case in her bag was the exact same case as mine, and then I understood that I had switched the contacts the night before.

After breakfast, we sorted out whose lenses were whose, and laughed at how funny it was that, despite having the same case and similar-looking lenses, neither of us could see through the other's contact lenses. It made me wonder, with our human eyes that all have lids, whites, irises, pupils and lashes, even when we look at the same world, what lens do we use to see that world? How might the world look different if we use a different lens?

THE BIRD DOESN'T STOP SINGING

I woke to the sound of a bird singing a sweet song. The chirping was lovely and I thought how wonderful it would be to sleep in this space and wake every morning to this sound. I looked at the clock and it was only 6 a.m. Having nothing to get up for, I rolled over and tried to go back to sleep, listening to the gentle singing of the bird. Then it became annoying. It wouldn't stop! I wished I had earplugs or something to shut the darn bird up. It had blissfully woken me, but now I wanted to sleep. Pesky bird! Oh wait. I love birds. I used to have birds as pets. I love their wings and their ability to fly, and think of myself as flying when my own legs won't support me, or when my ideas cannot be contained in my body. But right here, right now, I don't want the bird's song. I just want to roll over and go to sleep. The bird, knowing only its freedom and joy, doesn't stop singing.

LONELINESS

Am I in pain or am I paining? Pain coils around my heart like a snake, squeezing the joy and the gain out of that organ as if it were a dishrag. It hurts to be in my own skin. Five years ago at age 52, I sat in this very seat, with my husband in one room and my daughter in the other, secure in how my life was unfolding. The past and all its struggle was behind me; I looked forward to the future of an empty nest and the transformation it would bring in my relationship with Michael.

Transformation came, but not as I had expected. Here I sit now at 57, alone. It seems like I have lived several lifetimes and I know I cannot return to any of them, except in memory. The pang of loneliness has taken up residence in my chest, and I am familiar with its presence, not just from the years since Michael died, but also from the years before I met him. It occurs to me that this may be the best time of my life. There is much to celebrate in being alone, and much I enjoy about it. It has a freedom to it, as well as a sense of fear.

Tonight for the first time since Michael died, I put my wedding ring back on the fourth finger of my left hand. It feels foreign now. It feels too tight and constricting and does not belong there. Even seeing it as I write, it looks bizarre, incongruous, no longer my identifier. This fourth finger connected to my heart has changed. I look to the past to remind me how far I have come, to remind me that this present moment may be all I have, and there is no guarantee that the tomorrow I hope for will come. Silently, I take the ring off; gently, I put it on the table beside me, and it makes a little hollow clinking sound. Hollow. The pain eases a little but remains. I am learning to accept it and even to cherish it, for just like joy, it informs me that I am alive. It may be the best companion I could ever wish for.

OVERCOMING FEARS AND
SWIMMING WITH SHADOW

No one taught me to swim. Growing up in the English countryside, I rarely saw the beach. My first encounter with swimming in the ocean was at eight years of age. My foster mother walked with me into the ocean until I was beyond my depth. She then held me horizontally in the water, let go and said, "Swim!" I felt like I was sinking, so I flailed and struggled and choked. I was terrified as the water entered my lungs and I felt like I was drowning. She fished me out of the water, took me back to where I could stand on my own two feet and said, "You sank like a stone! Even if you do nothing, you can always float!" She was determined, and she took me back beyond my depth again. I wanted to please her, and I wanted so much to swim, but again, I sank and flailed and experienced that terror. I didn't trust that she would save me. My foster brother, almost three years my junior with more body fat than me, laughed at me as he happily floated on the ocean waves. I decided then that I would never venture out in the ocean again beyond my depth.

School provided swimming lessons for a few weeks a year in an icily cold outdoor swimming pool. I always stayed in the shallow end, and I always used a floating device. One day, after much ridicule by my peers, I decided I would let go of the floating device and copy the arm motions of the other children, and found that I could indeed swim and keep myself afloat for short periods of time. I never ventured out of my comfort zone, however. I made sure that I was never beyond my depth, and that at any time my feet could touch the ground. Later in life, I traveled to all sorts of destinations. I spent some summers with my cousins in Boston, who taught me to float and ride on waves on Nantasket Beach. I learned to watch for the big waves and the little ripples. I paddled my feet in the ocean in Israel, and floated in the Dead Sea. Always, I stayed within my comfort zone.

Forty-seven years later, I went for the first time to Kauai, Hawaii. From the moment the plane touched down, I could feel that there was something different about the atmosphere of this place. The sky seemed bigger and more open, the air clearer. It felt spiritual and magical. With a few hours to wait for one of my Esalen friends who would be sharing this vacation with me, I went to a beach near the airport. Although the beach was deserted, as I walked along the beautiful sand, I did not feel alone. It was as if my angels were whispering to me, and I sensed there was something about to happen that would change me.

My friends Christen and Jen and I rented a condo in Kauai that had its own private beach. They were wonderful swimmers and snorkelers. On the very first day, we went to the beach and they happily swam out in the water. I stayed behind, careful to make sure that I did not go where my feet could not touch ground. The sand was different than any I had encountered. The water was clear and I could see the ocean floor. As the waves came to shore, the sand seemed to pull me in, and I would fall and roll as the water lapped over me. My friends called to me, and I swam out to them. Before long, I was out of my depth, and swimming, staying afloat by the use of my arms and legs. When we went to a part of the ocean where we could stand and talk, I started to laugh and cry at the same time. I shared with them that this was the first time in forty-seven years I had swum in the ocean. It was a revelation to me, and liberating. Everything is possible!

The next morning, we met with Lauren, another Esalen friend who lives in Hanalei. Lauren surfs, has written a book about surfing, and has a Jack Russell Terrier named Shadow who surfs with her. There I was, confronted with another major fear of mine: Dogs. Anyone who knows me knows that I avoid dogs like the plague. If someone would not put their dog in another room when I visited them, I would not enter the house. If I saw a dog on the street that was not on a leash, I would turn around and go out of my way to avoid them. It wasn't that I hated dogs. I was terrified of being bitten by them. I had generalized my fear to include even the most docile of dogs. And here was Shadow. Lauren held him and I took a deep breath. Like swimming in the ocean, I went beyond my depth and reached out to stroke Shadow. When I touched him, my hands felt a warmth that was emotional in nature. I connected with Shadow as if he were a human being. Lauren got in her truck, followed by Shadow, and took us to the beach along with surfboards and rash guards. There, she taught us to surf. She told us that if we were to fall off the surfboard, we should not fight, but instead, relax and surrender to the water.

As I stood on the beach listening to Lauren, I was interrupted by a call informing me that a close coworker's husband had passed away. I took a walk along the beach to contemplate and to call my coworker. Breathing deeply after the call, I called my son-in-law to sing "Happy Birthday" to him. Two days prior I had congratulated a former student on the birth of her son, and on the same day had sent a basket of fruit to my mentor who had lost a family member. I felt privileged to be present even in a small way with all these life events. I looked out at my friends already surfing in the ocean, along with Shadow at the helm of the surfboard, and I joined them. I swam out, way beyond my depth, and when I wasn't surfing, I was bobbing in the ocean, arms outstretched to the sky, deeply grateful for the ocean and its depth and the expansiveness of my soul.

Later, when we went hiking on the Nā Pali trail, I would take Shadow in my arms and feel the beat of his heart against my chest, and a connection as he snuggled his head into my neck. I delighted in Shadow's company as we climbed over rocks, and again when I went snorkeling for the first time and saw the most beautiful sea life I would have missed had I stayed within my comfort zone and not ventured out of my depth. I am now able to be around dogs, and finally understand why many consider them Man's best friend.

It was no accident that Shadow came into my life at the same time I was shown how to ride the waves and to surrender to the water when I fall off the surfboard.

MOUNT MORIAH

My second grandson is named after Michael. I met Michael in Israel in 1975. On my grandson's first birthday, I journeyed back to Israel and stood on the Tayelet, a high vantage point looking out over the city of Jerusalem toward Mount Moriah. Mount Moriah is the place where the Bible says Abraham was supposed to have sacrificed his son Isaac, and the place where King Solomon built the Holy Temple. I stood there thinking about the last time I had journeyed there, just 12 weeks after Michael's death, and recognized how much healing had taken place in three years. Mount Moriah whispered to me, "Faith. Unshakable faith in the Master of the Universe has brought you to this moment."

DUST TO DUST

Walking through a forest of trees, you see those that are burned or have been cut down, those that are brittle and lifeless. They are the remnant of what they used to be, and yet they ceded to the earth a new life when they died. Once while hiking on a trail, I noticed a sign that read: "Downed trees are one of the greatest resources of the forest. The slow decomposition of the wood may take up to 500 years to 'melt' back into the soil. Meanwhile the log provides: Nesting places, hiding places, perches, food, colonization sites for termites, carpenter ants and beetles, fungi—an important food for wildlife. The downed trees in a forest are as valuable as standing trees." What a metaphor! From dust we came and to dust we will return, part of the lifecycle of the greater universe. Before we return to dust, and as part of the journey of that return, we must let go of our connections, hopefully in a way that is meaningful to the one departing as well as to the one who continues on their journey. How did they contribute to that journey? Let them know. What image comes to your mind when you think of them?

FOR EVERY END, THERE IS A BEGINNING

WHEN WORDS FAIL

When words fail me, what language shall I use? How shall I speak? Speech is not one of the senses. We hear, we see, we smell, we touch, we taste, but speech is not a sense, and yet we touch people with our words and our voice.

Words are important. It is at those times when words fail me that I am reminded that silence has so much power in it. It is in the silence that you can hear the whisper of Spirit, who uses the language of images rather than words. Those images can be transmitted through the eyes. With no words, the eyes can speak more eloquently than the mouth, and the mouth whose lips form the words, can in itself create images and expressions just by how it is moved.

When words fail me, what do I see? With my feeling eyes I see a countless range of emotions and textures, among them beauty, pain, longing and vulnerability. It is in the act of being vulnerable that I expose my world beyond words to another and I can reach out to touch them. In the touch of my hand, I can see the images and feel the words.

Thank you; will you forgive me? I forgive you; I love you; goodbye. All can be said without words, in the language of the senses, when words fail.

WALK FORWARD

I will end as I began, by asking you to please know that you have all the answers inside you. It is the questions that are important and the conversation that you have with yourself, past, present and future, which will determine the road your feet will walk on and the wings your spirit will use to fly. In the seminar I took with David Whyte, he asked us to ponder this question: "What is the courageous question that your future self will look back on and thank you for?"

Tending to the dying can be exhausting and also the most meaningful experience you will ever have. May you find peace in the present moment, ride the waves as they come, know that you are not alone, and that you are loved, no matter what.

RESOURCES

Thank you for joining me on this journey through this little handbook. I know that you may have many more questions that come up as you continue on this journey. Below is a list of the professional people and organizations that I have found helpful on my journey. Please feel free to share your story with me, or a resource that I may pass on to others through my website:

www.CantorSue.com

Esalen Institute	www.esalen.org
Hollyhock	www.hollyhock.ca
Bev Martin	www.bevmartin.com
Dr. Maria Sirois	www.mariasirois.com
Dr. Rick Jarow	www.rickjarow.com
Soaring Spirits Loss Foundation	www.sslf.org
Cantors Assembly	www.cantors.org
Rabbi Elie Spitz	www.cbi18.org
Vitas Hospice	www.vitas.com
David Whyte	www.davidwhyte.com

ACKNOWLEDGEMENTS

I owe deep gratitude to so many people who helped to bring this book about. For the love and devotion of my late husband Michael, who even in death gifted me with life, and my children, Edward, William, and Alexandra, along with their spouses, Ginna, Elana, and James, who teach me every day about gratitude, forgiveness, love, and letting go. The artwork in the book itself is drawn by William, and I would have chosen his work even if he were not my son. I stand on the shoulders of those who came before me: my uncle, David Gordon, my first father figure who I model my courage upon; my mother, Maureen Knight, who by her absence taught me about the importance of being present; my foster family Fachler, who give me anchor. On my way to becoming a Cantor, I am grateful for the mentorship of Cantor Nathan Lam, whose teaching and guidance forms the basis of my ministry, and who shows me opportunity when I might not see it; Cantor Shulamith Kalir-Merton who showed me how to find my path; Cantor Josef Chazan, who gave me my first opportunity to sing on the pulpit; and Rabbis Bradley Shavit Artson, Martin J. Cohen, Bernie King and Elie Spitz, who taught me how to live my Judaism authentically. Rabbi David Stein, who even in his last days of life gave his precious time, energy, and guidance on the stories in this book, and by responding to my singing showed me the power in it. The entire Cantors Assembly supports me in my sacred work, as well as the Institute for Jewish Spirituality. I offer thanks to the residents and staff of Heritage Pointe, with whom I have found meaningful work over fifteen years.

Directly involved with the book itself, and without whom there would be no book, is a long list of people to whom "thank you" barely expresses the depth of my gratitude. Dr. Adam Kendall, who taught me the discussions to have with Michael before he died, which became the basis for this work. The Auntie of the book, the intuitive Bev Martin, who "saw" the book before I did, and gave and continues to give generously of her time, love, spirit, deep listening, coaching and loving support. I cannot imagine either the conception or birth of the book without her. She inspires me. My two wonderful developmental editors, Cecilia and Jeff Starin, who tirelessly and lovingly read the manuscript over and over, standing in the place of the reader, recommended changes, and led me to my talented web designer and book cover designer, Charlotte Proud. My friends Marlene and Ed Ruden, for their friendship, support, and haven in Portland while I worked on the book. My friend Suzanne G. Mazel, who has listened to me several days a week for several years, even though I live in California and she in New York. Sue Artof, who gave me the confidence to go ahead and publish when I hit a wall with the manuscript. As this is my first book, having Abigail Carter take me by the hand and lead the way through the beginning process and timeline in the overwhelming world of self-publishing as well as finding my copy editor Megan Kinkade was invaluable and calming. For his expertise, speed, and generosity in formatting the book, all with an infectious laugh and solid advice, I am eternally grateful to Dan Clements. Understanding the quality of book I had in mind, I am indebted to Jerry Anderson of Headline Graphics, who worked hard to produce the printed version I envisioned.

The Esalen Institute, its staff, workshop leaders and seminarians have given me a place to come home to myself and continue to inspire me and be my haven. Particularly Dr. Maria Sirois, who so spearheaded my transformation that I followed her to Hollyhock, another haven in another country, and whose positive psychology model teaches me that I am worthy; and Dr. Rick Jarow, who taught me how to meditate, and whose spiritual and practical teaching and guidance teaches me to focus on what is important now. They were preceded in guidance by another mentor, Vince McCullough, who taught me my daily practice of yoga, that energy follows thought, and so much more that forms the basis of how I move in the world.

There are many others whose names could form a book in itself, to them, and to my unseen guides, I am grateful for your presence in my life and grace in the world.

Sue Knight Deutsch

Notes: